# RHYMES
## from the
# HINTERLAND

## Guy Graybill

BROWN POSEY PRESS

an imprint of Sunbury Press, Inc.
Mechanicsburg, PA USA

For information about special discounts for bulk purchases, please contact Sunbury Press Orders Dept. at (855) 338-8359 or orders@sunburypress.com.

To request one of our authors for speaking engagements or book signings, please contact Sunbury Press Publicity Dept. at publicity@sunburypress.com.

FIRST BROWN POSEY PRESS EDITION:  October 2025

Set in Adobe Garamond Pro | Interior design by Crystal Devine | Cover by Lawrence Knorr | Edited by Lawrence Knorr.

Publisher's Cataloging-in-Publication Data
Names: Graybill, Guy, author.
Title: Rhymes from the hinterland / Guy Graybill.
Description: First trade paperback edition. | Mechanicsburg, PA : Brown Posey Press, 2025.
Summary: A unique variety of poems, written over the past seven decades; with several appearing in a variety of U.S. and British publications and in an early book of the author's work, *Whimsy and Wry*, which contained essays, poems and a novella.
Identifiers: ISBN : 979-8-88819-416-4 (paperback).
Subjects: POETRY / American / General | POETRY / Subjects & Themes / General.

Designed in the USA
0  1  1  2  3  5  8  13  21  34  55

*For the Love of Books!*

This book is dedicated to Barbara Ann Staschiak, my dear companion of recent years, and to my daughter, Sonia Graybill; without whom the contents of this book would still be nothing more than scattered computer files.

# Contents

# FOREWORD

*By Jane and John Moore*

If you think poems should rhyme, you will appreciate Guy Graybill's *Rhymes from the Hinterland*. His poems rhyme. Guy's collection of 109 poems varies from short, whimsical pieces such as the four-line "Coy" to the much longer, 85-stanza "Rahab's Sisters," a serious musing about prostitution.

The author is thoughtful enough to explain to the reader who Rahab is at the beginning of the poem. That is helpful. But have a dictionary or your smart phone handy to look up some words. Guy accesses his wide knowledge of history and language when writing, and not all readers will know everything that Guy knows.

History-minded readers may know Guy best as the author of *Prohibition's Prince*, an entertaining biography of Pennsylvania's colorful moonshiner and bootlegger, Prince David Farrington. The book is a highly readable, fact-filled work of non-fiction.

We have known Guy for at least 30 years. He was Jane's coworker at Geisinger Medical Center where they were both medical transcriptionists. Transcriptionists had to qualify through a rigorous test to even begin the required training. John was an editor at the local newspaper when Guy was a Snyder County commissioner.

Imagine our surprise in encountering Guy as author of these poems—some light-hearted; others quite somber.

Who could resist the four short, humorous lines of "Befuddled?" Compare this poem with "Isle of Light," a serious work about the bombing of Hiroshima in 1945. It ends, "As decades drop behind us, the bomb begins to bore, / As 'just another weapon,' in 'just another war.' "

Rhymes includes a poem that's a word puzzle, "A Host of Jacks." There is a note before the poem, explaining what the reader can expect to find in the poem. (Jane: I had to think hard and refer to Google to find many of the references to Jacks, but I do not think I found them all.)

"Overheard At Lillian's Cotillion," a collection of near-homophones, will surely delight amateur linguists.

Some of the poems are historical or political. "Ode to Mary Jo" is about Mary Jo Kopechne's death in Teddy Kennedy's car.

Another historical poem is simply titled "Priestley." It's a biographical piece about Joseph Priestley, the British clergyman, author and scientist who moved to Northumberland, Pa., in self-imposed exile in 1794.

Priestley left England after a mob had burned his home in Birmingham. Noting the dangers inherent in 18th century oceanic travel, the poem observes, "Far safer is the raging sea/ Than where a riot may occur."

We enjoyed these poems and are pleased to help in introducing Guy's book of verse. There's something here for everyone.

# THE BRITISH MUSEUM

The best sources repeat it, unending,
For the scholars in ev'ry lyceum:
Many art works, of nations unlending,
Can be found in the British Museum.

There are statues and weapons and baskets,
Which could fill the entire Colosseum;
Plus amphoras and armor and caskets.
All are found in the British Museum.

They stole art works on ev'ry excursion.
Each success earned a joyful "Te Deum!"
All the booty, Egyptian or Persian,
Was displayed in the British Museum.

Woodblock prints of old Nippon are marvels;
But, don't go to Osaka to see 'em.
'Tho they capture Japan's unique beauty;
They, too, rest in the British Museum!

There's no doubt, if the Britons had found one—
A preserved, ancient peritoneum—
Though the practice may seem an unsound one,
It would lie in the British Museum!

Since old England has slowly been dying,
It will soon need its own mausoleum.
Then we'll learn, though without really trying,
England's now in the British Museum!

# YIN AND YANG

Yin and yang; dark and light;
Ice and fire: day and night.
Storm and calm; land and sea.
You and me . . . you and me.

Dual roles Nature gives;
Each upon the other lives.
Summit, vale; old and new;
Me and you . . . me and you . . .

Silence, sound; wet and dry;
Hate and love; earth and sky.
Both distinct, ever two;
Except us: Me and you . . .

# BATTLES

The most ancient of histories and hoariest tomes,
Tell us stories of men who abandoned their homes,
To go marching to conquer, in war after war.
All went forth, just to slaughter, in battles galore!

Wars began over comments or simply from fear,
While the reason for one was a man's severed ear.
Some were fought over bound'ries and some due to greed,
Though they all claimed to fight for a critical need.

They have fought on the waves and fought in the air,
Plus the ones without record, we know not just where.
They have battled in tundra and battled in sand.
They have battled in every inhabited land!

While some battles were epic, some others were small.
Many raged in the spring; others raged in the fall.
Some were fought in the heat of the midsummer day;
Thus increasing the speed of gangrene and decay.

Countless souls were consumed by the madness so rife!
Countless limbs were cut free by the surgeon's sharp knife.
Countless heads were removed by the cannonball's flight.
Hardened men whispered prayers in the dead of the night.

They would fight in retreat and in foolhardy drives,
And they lived with the horror the rest of their lives.
They would sleep to escape from the guns and the screams;
But the fiends from the battlefield haunted their dreams!

They left graves for the masses and graves for the lone,
And graves, as memorials, to corpses unknown.
They left bodies in snowdrifts and bodies in bogs.
They left corpses as food for the ravens and dogs.

Some folks love to suggest that we learn from the past.
They say wars teach us lessons that help us recast.
But, my own observation comes laden with gall:
If there's one thing we learn, we learn nothing at all!

# HAND-ME-DOWNS

Thru the small pantry window he watched them;
Through the fast-fading light of the day.
He observed, with affection, his children,
Walking home from their school, miles away.

First, the tall, teen-aged son crossed the barnyard,
Just ahead of the daughter, his twin.
Then the eight-year-old son came-a-straggling.
All arrived at their house, then went in.

Empty lunch pails they sat on the table,
While their ma greeted each one in turn.
They laid books, to be studied by lantern,
On the bench, where they'd soon sit to learn.

As their father stepped into the kitchen,
All three joined him to walk to the barn;
But the younger son tugged at his jacket
And recited a child's touching yarn.
The old teacher, the child told his father,
That old spinster who lives in the town,
Made him stand 'fore the class as she told them
All his clothing had been 'handed down'.

Giggling 'rose as she spoke, he related;
As she said that each item he wore
Had been there, in her room, on his brother.
She had " 'taught' all his clothing before!"

Now the father's rough fingers were gentle,
As they brushed youthful tears from a cheek.
Then he stood with his son by the barn door
And reflected, before he would speak.

The two stood for long moments in silence
As the father prepared what to say.
Then he rested his hand on a shoulder
And spoke, in a fatherly way.

"Do you know that this farm where we're living
Was passed down by my granddad to me?
'Though it's small, it's got fine, fertile soil
And our house is delightful to see!"

"And your mother's fine set of bone china;
Handed down from her mother to her.
But, it's not just material possessions,
Where the hand-me-downs often occur."

"Didn't teacher once say you were clever,
With a mind that was witty and fine?
Well, your wit you have gained from your mother,
'Though I'd hope that a little was mine."

"Now, your eyes? Hand-me-downs from your grandma
And your smile was my dad's truth to tell.
We are all hand-me-downs, of a fashion,
In our minds and our bodies as well."

"So, my son, just as long as you're honest
And as kind as we've taught you to be;
Then don't mind that possessions aren't recent.
If they serve you: That's really the key!

"Now, be quick to go help with the barn work,
'Cause your mother's made supper by now."
Then the father walked down to the stables,
While his son threw down hay from the mow.

As he worked, a chill wind swirled about him,
So he buttoned his hand-me-down coat;
And it promptly began to protect him,
From a world far too cold . . . and remote.

# ISLE OF LIGHT

As ancient tribal bowmen might fight a bowless band,
A nation's modern weapon can crush a weaker land.
Upon a distant island, a plane was set on course;
Within, unseen in warfare, a new and Hellish force!

The plane droned through the darkness; its crew a chosen few.
They flew above the ocean; a somber, starlit view.
Within the target city, no one foresaw the guest.
Most rose to greet the new day; while slumber held the rest. . . .

But, then arose a thousand suns; one blinding, searing flash!
What Twilight bathed in glory, foul Dawn would bathe in ash!
The victors won their skirmish, with soldiers undeployed.
They also won their battle. The vanquished were destroyed.

That bomb destroyed an empire. Proud leaders had to bow.
But, that is all behind us; for we are here and now.
Soon, other nations differed and later wars were waged.
Old conflicts are forgotten; Fate's diary must be paged.

My sadness overwhelms me. My sorrow overcomes,
As I recall how fickle we're made by martial drums.
As decades drop behind us, *the bomb* begins to bore,
As 'just another weapon,' in 'just another war'. . . .

# McCLAY'S HOLLOW

*(Written as Bluegrass lyrics)*

1.

We was married on a mountain
On a foggy Saturday
And we lived deep in that mountain
In a hollow called McClay.

2.

We McClays was first to settle
And the only folks to stay
By the stream that formed the hollow;
Formed the hollow called McClay.

3.

All we done we done together,
From the day she took my name.
Side by side we walked my trap line.
Side by side we hunted game.

4.

She would keep the flame a burnin'
When we fired our little still
And she filled the jars with moonshine
That we hid behind the hill.

5

Late at night she'd still be quilting,
Earnin' money for our purse.
We'd both till our stony garden
Tho' she chided when I'd curse.

CHORUS
*I've been plannin' on returnin'*
*To the hollow called McClay*
*Really plannin' to go back there*
*When my sorrow goes away.*

6.
We was happy in our cabin
In the hollow called McClay
And she cried with joy on learnin'
She was in the fam'ly way!

7.
She was always skeered o' crossin
That old bridge that Pappy made;
But I told her not to worry . . .
That she needn't be afraid.

8.
Then one night we hurried homeward
'Cause we heard the thunderclaps.
She had just stepped on the footbridge
When I saw the bridge collapse!

9
How she screamed as she was fallin'
Down into the rocky stream!
Just a second's deadly silence . . .
Until I began to scream!

10
She was buried with our unborn
On a foggy Saturday
In that rocky little graveyard
Of the family named McClay.
(Chorus)

11
I took chisel to a fieldstone
For a marker for their grave.
All the while I was a cryin'
Knowin' all the love she gave.

12
Twenty two miles through the mountains
To her fam'ly's house I walked.
Told them of their daughter's dyin';
So choked up I barely talked.

13
In my sadness, I decided
That I wanted far away
From the cabin, and the graveyard
And the hollow called McClay.

14
So I walked out of those mountains
To the city where I stay.
While her grave remains untended
And the cabin rots away.

15

Seven years I've been a grievin'
Seven years, and still I roam.
'Though I try, I still can't do it;
Can't forget our mountain home.


Chorus
Yes, I'm plannin' on returnin'
When my sorrow goes away . . .
To be buried there, beside her,
In the hollow called McClay.

# OF ALL THE DWELLINGS IN THIS WORLD

With buyer's offer now the case,
You'll soon require a dwelling place.
Of all the dwellings, Maine to Nome,
Which single one has traits of home?

Of all the dwellings in this world,
In which have You found Love, unfurled?
In which have we, our longings bared?
In which have we, some passions, shared?

Here sits the home where lips were pressed
To kindle flames of two, obsessed!
Will you explain why we demurred?
Must we pretend no love occurred?

Of furnishings now resting here,
I'll switch three quarters, for you, Dear!
Where possible, I'll walk the stairs,
As favors giv'n from one who cares.

With all this home's brick wall encase,
I'll cede to you o'er half the space!
Declaring that I'll stay the gent,
No money will you owe in rent.

Your smile will be the rental fee.
Your kisses match the equity.
Our Love began with that first kiss,
Let's nudge it toward a greater bliss!

# A GLORIOUS SIGHT

Before our liberty was gained,
Our rebel forbears clearly knew
An emblem had to be obtained.
They fashioned one: red, white and blue.
It led them into battle's hell
And on to vict'ry in their fight.
Their spirits must be proud to know:
Old Glory's still a precious sight.

We see our flag in small parades,
Where aging veterans raise it high.
We see it on the courthouse roof;
A'fluttering against the sky.
It waves above our nation's dome;
It's presence there is our delight;
Reminding us, as we move on:
Old Glory's still a joyful sight.

Its stripes and stars bring out our best:
Inspiring songs and rhymes and deeds.
It tells us we must live as one,
Without regard for varied creeds.
Don't wrap injustice in our flag
Or hide aggression as we might.
Be sure our young can say with pride:
"Old Glory's still a thrilling sight!"

Now, tug the rope and raise the flag
Into the morning's rosy light.
Then watch a breeze unfurl the folds.
Old Glory's still a glorious sight!

# HIDDEN TREA$URE

I saved my shiny pennies when I was just a kid.
I placed them in containers . . . tin boxes that I hid.
Some pennies came as payment for jobs which I'd complete
I found some at the fairgrounds, as well as on the street.
Strict saving makes the miser, and that's what I became.
I wouldn't purchase candies; I never bought a game!
My pennies grew in number; the tins piled, one on one.
My childhood goals were focused. My fortune was begun.
Times turning has been rapid. The years have slipped away.
My pennies stayed in storage, until one recent day.
I gathered all my pennies into a heavy sack,
Then went to see the banker, my coins upon my back.
When all my loot was counted, the tally was a shock!
Dismayed, I eyed my money, devalued by the clock.
My sacrifice in childhood, to scrimp and save and horde,
Was gutted by inflation, that economic sword!
I should have bought some candy, at Abner's corner store,
Or bought a gift for Grandma, or wined the girl next door.
I took my paltry pittance and exited the bank.
Then strolled the sidewalk wond'ring how my investment shrank.
Just as I turned a corner, an antique shop I spied.
An object in the window caused me to rush inside!
A tin of faded label, but salty in the cost,
Matched hundreds which I'd stockpiled! My effort *wasn't* lost.
What seems a prize at present, may be a waste to hold;
But trash, today discarded, may be tomorrow's gold!

# MALDA LAUDED

Oh, Malda! Malda! Dear Ms. Hyde!
Her features cannot be denied!
She's made me now so starry-eyed,
That, of myself, I am beside!

Temptations, which I can't abide,
Would have me toss all shame aside!
My honor . . . dignity . . . and pride:
I'd lose them all for Malda Hyde!

# COY

Some men will boast of prowess, great.
Methinks they may exaggerate.

I've matched their feats a thousand times;
But, only in my thoughts and rhymes.

# A HOST OF JACKS

~ A note about *A Host of Jacks* ~

The name, 'Jack', must be the most widely-used name in the English-speaking world for identifying all sorts of objects and ideas. The following poem—*A Host of Jacks*—obliquely identifies only about half of those uses. The rhyme is in the form of a quiz. Beginning with the fourth verse, the reader should identify two distinct applications of 'Jack' in each verse, except the final one, which has but one reference.

1.
When you say your name's 'Jack', don't expect me to know
Just which Jack, of all Jacks, that you are.
Don't you know I've found Jacks everywhere that I've been?
Jack's a name that appears near and far.

2.
It's a maddening thing; yes, a maddening thing,
Having Jacks start to clutter my mind.
It's as though some mad witch cast your name to the winds,
As a way to confound humankind!

3.
So, please listen to me as I hasten to ask,
What's the trick to your name? Where's the clue?
Let me guess several Jacks. When I guess the right one,
Kindly tell me the Jack that is you.

4.
Are you jack who can work just about any task
And can wear, as it were, many caps?
Or, do you live the rhyme where you dine with your spouse,
With your plate left devoid of all scraps?

5.
But, perhaps you're the game that involves no last name;
Only pieces and high-bouncing ball?
Better still, are you Jack that's pure lead in a wrap,
That can easily bludgeon a skull?

6.
Are you Jack of the fields; the one hunters pursue
And with offspring galore, near and far?
Or will you, with one arm, the lone arm that you own,
Dare to lift the one end of a car?

7.
Did you build the famed structure, whose story then tells
Of a rodent and one crooked horn;
Or are you what inspires so much grand 'Limey' pride,
As you wave from the pole where you're borne?

8.
Are you, Jack, who gives sermons, both flow'ry and fresh,
Standing solemn and lacking a smile;
Or the one all help build, where the ante resides,
With but one likely winning the pile?

9.
Are you Jack, who can smile, mouth and eyes all aglow,
As your pulpy head makes children yell;
Or the Jack badly hurt from the tumble you took,
As you tried to return from the well?

10.
Are you popcorn and peanuts that come with a toy,
In a box you can buy at the mart;
Or the seasonal Jack, who plucked fruit from his dish,
While he dined all alone on a tart?

11.
Are you tall, always green, and a needler of sorts;
One who thrives on a cold, windy hill?
Or do you climb and climb toward the loftiest goal,
Just to flee from a giant, most shrill?

12.
Are you cider that passed to a much higher state,
That will make steady men sway and lurch?
Or are you such a one as will work near the sky,
While repairing or painting a church?

13.
Say, do you chatter loudly, in rough, steady hands,
Cracking stone and removing our street?
Or do you roam at night through the fog-shrouded slums,
Where you might disembowel those you meet?

14.
Do you stay by the door so our footwear gets cleaned,
Helping keep domiciles span and spick;
Or, reversing your name, are you martial and vain;
Rattling nerves, as your partner you click?

15.

Do you try dang'rous games, where you're playing with fire,
With a leap that might end in the dark;
Or were you once a pup; but now grown to a dog,
With short hairs and cacophonous bark?

16.

Do you send a cold chill down my spine when we meet,
As, in fact, you might freeze all in sight;
Or, are you the old tool with the mid-folding blade,
Whose mere presence is cause for some fright?

17.

Are you crow's smaller brother with gold amid green,
And 'grackle' an alias you use;
Or the odd, little man who will spring to surprise,
As a plaything designed to amuse?

18.

Are you Jack who fells trees on the larch-covered ridge,
And who teeters on logs in the bay?
Or have you royal blood, with four monarchs at hand,
And, sometimes just one eye to display?

19.

Why, of course! With that crown, I should surely have known.
It's with you that romance always starts.
You're the symbol of Love, who's escaped from the deck.
You're the one known to all: Jack of Hearts!

# ANCESTORS FORLORN

From elderly to youngest child,
Methinks our forebears never smiled!
It seems that ev'ry picture shows
Each person with a solemn pose!

When shutters snapped and powder flashed,
All faces froze! All smiles were trashed!
No cheery smile was ever gleaned.
Was each upon a lemon weaned?

To young and old, to short and tall,
Photographers declared to all:
"All folk from farm, and those from town,
Alright now. . . . Everybody, FROWN!"

# OUR YOUNG

They are safe as they play
Here among us today;
But, how safe will they play
On the morrow;
Since the strangers came in,
With a smile and a grin,
Thus to buy
What they never could borrow?

Using money and guile
And political style,
They got land
Which was prime and impressive.
Will our young ones soon shrink
From the water they drink,
'Cause the toxins within are excessive?

Will the strangers provide
Waste for making our wide
Susquehanna a river of sorrow?
They are safe as they play
Here among us today . . .
But, will they safely play
On the morrow?

# LIBERTY BELL

Two thousand pounds of fire-cast bronze
Above the city ringing;
Reverberating 'cross the roofs,
A novel notion bringing.

The clapper strikes the massive dome,
The crowd, below, rejoicing.
This bell's the nation's vocal chord.
Our Liberty it's voicing.

'Though hidden, briefly, from the foe,
Beneath a church's planking;
It joins the treasures of the free
And holds a lofty ranking.

It joins the Eagle and the Flag,
And documents, inspiring;
To help the nation stay alert,
While seeking Peace, untiring . . ..

Two thousand pounds of fire-cast bronze,
It sends the message ringing;
Reverberating 'cross the land,
To set a people singing!

# AN ACT OF SELF DEFENSE

Her Smile is a rebel Smile.

She knows the disarming art.

Her lips bring to light her guile:

A threat to my sov'reign heart.


Before my defiance slips,

I'll show that her threat is known.

I'll siege those rebellious lips,

To crush them beneath my own!

# BEFUDDLED?

With a never-present *future*
And a never-present *past;*
Be sure our present *present*
Will never, ever last!

# IN LAURA'S LAND

The trees still shade Wisconsin hills
And prairie grass grows wild . . . unplanned.
Cool waters flow within Plum Creek.
Not much has changed in Laura's Land!

In Walnut Grove a church bell rings.
Pa's money helped to buy the bell.
It's ringing floats across the plain
And 'cross the prairie years as well.

The old Surveyor's House remains.
The tiny Master's inn still stands;
And on the Kansas prairie is
The well Pa dug on Indian lands.

The cottonwoods Pa planted there
Stand strong out on his old tree claim.
Dakota winds are wild and free
As Laura was . . . too wild to tame!

As sunset fills the prairie sky
Then, surely you will understand.
You'll know the reason why you came
To see . . . and savor . . . Laura's Land.

# BURIAL AT SEA

*(Written before the passing of the late senator)*

Our nation's living dreadnought,
The champ of ocean sea,
Our legendary captain,
Horatio Kennedy!

Sea shanties praise his vict'ry
Along the Bay State's coast.
Of all his deeds, heroic,
This stirs our hearts the most.

By day he raced regatta
Aboard his trusty yacht.
Magnanimous while losing;
Our Yankee Lancelot.

It takes a stalwart husband
To leave his pregnant wife;
A truly flinty fellow,
To lead the playboy's life.

The post-regatta shindig
Had six females, unwed;
Plus six men, unrelated;
And that's including Ted.

The booze was freely stockpiled;
Enough to fill a cove.
Ted found a comely colleague.
Into the night they drove.

He raced with quick abandon
To reach a place he knew:
A spit of barren seashore,
Away from prying view.

An open bridge now looming;
The lass beside him, curled.
No way could he avoid it;
The splash heard 'round the world!

The speeding car plunged downward
Into the briny pool.
Heroically, he surfaced.
"Save Number One," the rule.

He bravely bypassed houses,
Where he might summon aid.
He hurried to his cohorts.
How bold and unafraid!

Some might still try to rescue.
For Ted, that wouldn't fit.
Of course, we're all agreeing:
Deserting takes more grit.

With courage, he kept silent
For nine hours, through the night;
Except to call for cronies
To help assess his plight.

To win that timeless battle,
Took brilliant plan and plot.
He lost but one companion:
She, whom the world forgot.

When he's no longer with us,
We'll hear the nation wail.
The mythic sea will take him.
His shroud cut from a sail.

Then, from the bridge we'll lower him.
To give the body weight,
We'll add a heavy object:
His black, Olds 88.

# ODE TO MARY JO

A curse on the unfeeling,
Who let the decades go
With indignation lacking.
No thoughts of Mary Jo

None cared about your rescue;
Just save the final son.
Before the sea engulfed you
The spinning had begun!

Your cause was never championed
By members of the press.
Police and prelates shying
For reasons one can guess.

They focused all the pity
On him who was to blame
And caused a thoughtless nation
To disregard your name.

To save his polished image
And prop his Public Life,
He must attend your funeral
With neckbrace and a wife.

The wife seemed as a robot,
With troubled, vacant look.
His neckbrace just as phony
As older brother's book!

I can't finance a statue;
But think you ought to know:
I still recall your horror!
I'm sorry . . . Mary Jo.

# THE ROMANCE OF WAR

Our young should know of war;
That pre-historic way
Men found to wound and slay . . .
To smear the land with gore!

Our young should early learn
That slaughter can be done
To groups, as well as one
No mercy to discern.

It might do well to teach
That twisted minds delight
In barbarism's sight;
'Though claims to 'order' preach!

To help our young ignore
The horror and the hell;
We've made a myth, and well:
The fine romance of war!

This knowledge to bestow,
We should, with passion, yearn.
War's TRUTH our young should learn:
But war they should not KNOW!

# COIN O' THE REALM

"Miss Maudie" ran a bawdy house
Beside a pike in country shire;
And there she kept a woolly ewe
That lusty rustics paid t' hire.

But, what th' price for tuppin';
Th' charge for knowin' ovine love?
A tuppence was 'er tuppin' fee.
An' not a ha' penny above!

# WINNOWING

We don't need the mice
An' we don't need rats.
If there are no mice,
We don't need the cats.
We don't need 'possum
An' we don't need hogs.
We don't need the ticks
Or the polliwogs.

We don't need roaches
An' we don't need bears.
We don't need spiders.
An' we don't need hares.
We don't need 'skeeters'
An' we don't need gnats.
Without them 'skeeters,'
We'll never need bats.

We don't need the wasps
Or the centipedes.
We don't need the sharks
Or the canine breeds.

We don't need tigers
An' we don't need fleas.
We need only us . . .
An' the honey bees.

# LIKE PURSUITS

*Shakelton in the Antarctic*
*Lewis and Clark in the Rockies*
*Mackenzie in the Canadian Northwest*
*Cook in the South Pacific*
*Burton and Speke in East Africa*
*Chapman in the Gobi*
*Me in the master bedroom*

# AN ARTIFICIAL RHYME?

The crocodile's renowned for his artificial tears,
While artists besmirch canvas with artificial smears
And leeching lords of England are artificial peers.
Curse tyrants who demand them; our artificial cheers!

In danger's path I'd welcome some artificial fears!
Know Samson was not shorn by some artificial shears.
I'd never stare at beauties with artificial leers,
Tho' women try to lure us, with artificial rears!

No monkey wrench will loosen some artificial gears
And, if my rhymes upset you, shout artificial jeers.
My age I keep a secret with artificial years.
Nor would I now offend you with artificial sneers.

Storms cannot launch a stampede with artificial steers
And natives did no fishing with artificial weirs.
Recruits are left to guzzle their artificial beers;
And Indian braves showed Custer no artificial spears!

THE HOLLYHOCK BALLET TROUPE

# A FERTILE FIELD

Across all climes,
Among all creeds:
Debunkers do
The noblest deeds!

# CENTURIES

*The fabled Nostradamus*
*Fooled simple-minded hacks,*
*With riddles that were riddled*
*With trash instead of facts.*

*Yet, ev'ry generation*
*Construes his mutant rhymes,*
*In ways that fit their motives*
*And seem to match the times.*

*The truly thoughtful person*
*Will always be content,*
*To save each grand prediction*
*'Til after the event.*

# THE VIGIL MAINTAIN

So, you've put away all of your armor.
So, your lance you have now set aside!
And you say we have slain all the dragons?
Here our thinking is bound to collide.

You're a fool, who is too soon deluded.
Our world's yet the dark, beast-laden wood.
Here live creatures that hope to devour us;
Here are foes who would do us no good.

They are cloaked in a guise that is modern—
Like the razor-sharp blade in the sheath—
So that, outwardly, they appear harmless;
But, the 'dragon' still lurks underneath!

Some are nations that feign would embrace us;
Others, groups that would offer us peace.
Some are concepts that promise Utopia . . .
The proverbial 'wolves under fleece'?

All those brutes would, with ease, overpower us,
If we fell, importunely, asleep.
So, we must have the moat filled with Caution
And let Truth help us strengthen the keep.

We've no choice but to maintain the vigil,
And be certain our young can derive
A concern for the imminent dangers.
The alert are the ones who survive!

# A PRIVILEGED FEW

A Latvian of seaside home
Is also known as 'Balt'.
While ev'ry fool, from pole to pole,
Is drawn into a cult.

The briny sea's not potable,
Because it's filled with salt,
And beer's a drink most popular,
Because it's laced with malt.

The Oregonians live in fear,
While sitting on a fault;
And movie fans again will cheer
By resurrecting Walt.

These facts are known to ev'ryone,
As though by some default;
Yet, none but doctors really know
When stool is in the vault.

# NOCTURN

Shadows on the wall . . .
Scribblings on the sheet.
Midnight came and went.
Silence in the street.

Night and solitude,
Soon release, for play,
Thoughts which always hide
From the light of day.

Nighttime does its work;
Asking, as its fee,
That the soul recall
Painful memory.

Solemn and alone,
Seated by the lamp,
Thoughts of old return,
Making eyes grow damp . . .

# OVERHEARD AT LILLIAN'S COTILLION

My teachers gave me ribbons
And trimmed me with medallions;
But, why did they not teach me
That quarts do not make galleons?

Within my font of knowledge,
I know that vain Italians
Will posture to convince us
That they are sturdy stallions.

If Gore could harvest onions
Would they be called Vidallions?
And were they in the kitchen
When scullions ate the scallions?

Sound money won't concern them;
Political reptilians.
They'll do it, willy-nilly:
Turn bullion into billions.

Yes, Britain's Crystal Palace,
With all its glass pavilions,
Might have enhanced its décor
With mullions by the millions . . .

# UPBRINGING

While I was yet an infant,
My parents cast the die.
They weaned me on bologna;
They fed me rabbit pie.

And as a lad, a-growing,
They gave me kettle meat,
Along with steaming mince pies,
Both savory and sweet.

They set my tastes forever
And didn't even try.
A carnivore they raised me;
A carnivore I'll die.

# THE RAIN

If I can know the roof won't leak
And drenching waters won't remain,
And know, as well, each drop's unique,
I love to see the rain.

If I can know the earth will drink
And plants will sprout where seeds have lain,
To help all life to interlink,
I love to smell the rain.

If I can find a sheltered seat,
As raindrops sound their blurred refrain,
My restful mood becomes complete.
I love to hear the rain.

If I can flout propriety
And eye convention with disdain;
And hear you say, "Come, walk with me,"
I love to feel the rain!

# WASATCH WHIMSY

The quilt maker thoughtfully
matches her patches.
The locksmith manipulates
catches and latches.

Ma Hen, on her eggs, always
hatches in batches
An old Irish bloke still
attaches the thatches.

A spy, most elusive, now
snatches dispatches.
For votes, ev'ry candidate
Scratches at klatches and
Our paddlewheel pilot
Detaches at Natchez.

# SUNRISE AND SADNESS

When hopes lie shattered on the shore,
Good friends are often wont to say:
"The Sun will rise; just as before.
Tomorrow is another day."
That's what good friends are wont to say.

But grave injustice came to call.
Yes, grave injustice came to stay.
So, I must dine on bitter gall
And I'm condemned to sip dismay,
No matter what good friends might say.

On days when duties don't impede,
My will can't push me from the cot.
If bladder does not intercede,
I'd rather slumber; rather rot,
Than join a world where truth's forgot!

I curse the knaves who gain success
By trampling ethics under hoof.
One thought ignites my bitterness:
I sense the crime; but lack the proof . . .
I sense the crime; but lack the proof.

To know injustice, unerased,
Leaves morning's joy forever gone;
With courage lost and hope effaced.
So long as justice is withdrawn,
Sunrise and sadness crow the dawn . . .

# AN ODIOUS ODE

O, bay; the horse on which we rode.
Obey, the essence of our code.

O, sage, the spice upon our meat.
Osage, the Native whom we greet.

O, bow, the warrior's hope in war.
Oboe, the music we deplore.

O, mitt, the catcher's trusty aid.
Omit, and leave the debt unpaid.

O, lay, the faithful evermore.
"Olé!" our shout to matador.

O, pine I, for my love's embrace.
Opine, I, to express my case.

O, void, my stomach's empty bin.
Ovoid, the eggs I cram therein.

O, bleak, the journey of a hearse.
Oblique, the angle of this verse.

# THE HYPOCRITES

They dot their ev'ry 'i'
And cross their ev'ry 't'.
They're perfect, so they claim,
Compared to you and me.

No rule may thus be bent
By any human known.
There's nothing they'll approve
And nothing they'll condone.

With knowledge less than slight,
They think they know too much;
So those they find know more
They claim are 'out-of-touch'.

Should ever you dispute
The power they've assumed,
There's none can stay your fate.
In wrath, you'll be consumed!

They summon all their friends,
To quickly congregate.
They made a super find:
Another group to hate!

With venom they condemn.
Each boldly vilifies;
With rumors lacking base
And oft-repeated lies.

At those who bend the rules,
They're first to cast a stone.
There's no exception seen
Except, of course, their own!

# DECORUM

Of all the traits which we've possessed,

Decorum rates among the best.

Propriety our shriek dilutes

And separates us from the brutes.

We know, of course, exceptions fit.

Sometimes decorum I'd omit;

And, "Dignity be damned," I say:

My little grandchild wants to play!

# DECEIVE ME

Please, deceive me. Make me think
That I'm charming, when I drink.
Let me tell myself once more
That I'm not a stumbling bore.
Both at home and where I work,
I'm no alcoholic jerk.

Please, deceive me. Tell me, clear,
I can handle kegs of beer
And, despite a slurring tongue,
I am never overhung;
I've not fallen off the page.
I'm a very lucid sage.

Please, deceive me, let me think
I can handle all I drink.
Help me tell myself, today,
That I'm sober as I lay
In the gutter, flask in hand.
Make me think that I can stand.

Please, deceive me. I'm convinced
That each time my children winced,
They still found me full of fun.
I need alcohol to run.
Sober is no way to be.
Booze, alone, will set me free!

# THE LINE DRAWN

I met a man of Marxist stripe,
While trav'ling Life's bleak road;
And, just as I, he'd sweat and thirst,
While hunger, too, he showed.

And when the sun, it's zenith reached,
We found some soothing shade.
We placed our rations on the ground,
Then, briefly, there parlayed.

"Now let us eat," he gently said,
And pulled the wine's small cork;
While I was quick in my reply:
"Now here, sir, have a fork."

And, though we spoke of thoughts we shared.
We were of different hue.
Too soon, I was dismayed to hear:
"You know, we'll BURY you!"

'Though much in common I had seen,
Compassion I'd displayed—
Yet, sure as Hell, I did not state:
"Now here, Sir, have a spade!"

# AM I YOUR LAST TATTOO?

Oh, Stan . . . you're such a handsome man!
I fell when we first kissed . . .
But, how'd you get so many names
Tattooed from neck to wrist!?

Although you said you'd love me, Sweet;
Forever and a day;
I've got this nagging thought, my pet.
That simply won't go 'way . . .

With Karen, Sharon, Jen and Ruth;
Plus Liz and Mary Sue,
Upon your husky arm displayed;
Am I your last tattoo?

You say my name will top them all:
Beyond Belle, Nell and Fawn.
You've "saved a place" that's just for me,
Above Kay, May and Dawn!

Of course, I shouldn't doubt your word.
I'm sure your love is true;
But, then I spy there, Meg and Peg. . . .
Am I your last tattoo?

Can we erase Lou Ann and Grace?
Although I mean no harm . . .
I'd love to see my name alone.
How can we clear your arm?

Right on your biceps, burn my name.
You know the honor's due.
Then I can brag to ev'ryone . . .
That I'm . . . your last . . . tattoo!

# RAHAB'S SISTERS

*The Biblical accounts tell us that* Rahab, *a harlot of Jericho, hid and protected two Israelite spies in order to save her family from the coming destruction of the town. The names of the two spies went unrecorded; but, after about 3,300 years,* Rahab's *name lingers.* Rahab *is, then, one of the world's oldest, named prostitutes. Today, more than three millennia later, prostitution thrives. It remains a money-driven, exploitative, disease-spreading form of degradation and servitude, catering ever to lust; never to love.*

I
Oh, dusky, Semite harlot,
Now dead three thousand years,
Too bad there are no ledgers,
That list your nameless peers.

II
But, Rahab, you're immortal.
Your name we'll always know.
You plied your trade by serving
The johns of Jericho.

III
You saved two spies from capture.
Their names are long forgot.
But you, Rahab, a strumpet
Have gained a heroine's slot.

IV
Was yours the first profession;
The oldest ever known?

Did it, with all its evils,
Spring from the earth, full blown?

V
While blowhards love to chortle,
They are but thoughtless 'simps'.
I say you were preceded
By 'mongers and by pimps!

VI
From tribes to modern nations,
In laws we put our trust;
Still, no decree yet written
Has moderated lust.

VII
Not all men paid for harlots.
Some priests of ancient lands,
Put whoring in the temples
To serve their own demands.

VIII
Old Sampson's head, thought Franklin,
Contained a mental gap;
Or else he'd not have laid it
Upon a harlot's lap.

IX
How rare to see a harlot
Escape her life, obscene.
Remember Theodora?
From courtesan to Queen!

X

When children joined a Crusade,
They reached a 'friendly' port.
The merchants there enslaved them,
To 'crusade' for men's sport.

XI

A wanton king of England
Kept two sluts to adore.
The one a wayward Catholic,
Plus Nell, 'the other whore'!

XII

Tho' Gladstone turned some strumpets
From your infernal trade,
It was as catching snowflakes;
The impact that he made.

XIII

Men, heartless and barbaric
Would comb the coastal ports;
Kidnaping doe-eyed daughters
Unhampered by the courts.

XIV

Mere youngsters joined the market
Their welfare was a sham.
Men sold them by the thousands,
To dens of old Siam

XV

Were you a camp-side hooker,
With Hay Street for your base?
Or did you work New Orleans
With syncopated grace?

XVI
Which ones were seeking freedom
From hearthside tyrants' rules,
When snared by preying panders
To be their human tools?

XVII
We've harlots of the body
And harlots of the mind.
Should those who sell their genius
Condemn the other kind?

XVIII
The whoring found in movies
Is nothing but veneer.
Films love to highlight glamour;
While hiding filth and fear.

XIX
How can you face the mirror?
Your life is all charade;
As gaudy paint and pretense
Identify your trade.

XX
You offer, as a bonus,
While men are in your arms,
Some very crippling microbes
To those who buy your charms.

XXI
The conference halls were busy
With men who fought the trade;
But, busier the brothels
Where fortunes could be made.

XXII
Your sister in Chicago
Betrayed her trusting mate.
Her outfit? Gaudy crimson.
An ambush sealed his fate!

XXIII
How many of your sisters
Found poverty the trail
That led to their becoming
As objects stripped for sale?

XXIV
Someone within your circle
Can claim Hell's legacy.
Who was the whore or whoreson
Who caught the first V.D.?

XXV
Is not the old contagion—
Along with others, new—
A risk with each new client;
For him, as well for you?

XXVI
Your body may be linking
A ghastly daisy chain.
From ancients it may carry
That first venereal strain.

XXVII
Old fears were surely reasoned.
T'was hell for all unspared.
Those damned syph'litic horrors,
Your sisters got and shared.

XXVIII
You spread the vile infection,
As pebbles in the pond.
The microbes traveled quickly.
Your illness had no bond.

XXIX
Great freighters left the harbors
With goods for distant shores;
The crewmen harb'ring microbes
Obtained from dock-side whores.

XXX
The laws regarding strumpets
Reflected all we've feared.
For all the laws enacted,
Great forests disappeared.

XXXI
When macho men, with swagger,
Went hankerin' after whores,
You'd see upon each visage
The chancres and the sores.

XXXII
Of whoredom's dread diseases,
Don't ever claim you're free,
Since any new encounter
Must void the guarantee!

XXXIII
I've never had a chancre
Or ever had a sore;
And since I never want one,
I'd never hug a whore.

XXXIV
Do clients ever offer
A word of sympathy?
Is homage ever offered,
Beyond the strumpet's fee?

XXXV
Now, here's a valid statement:
A fact you can't ignore.
No matter what the statute,
A whore is still . . . a whore.

XXXVI
You are a walking leper.
Disease in you is rife.
T'will pass again, sans warning,
To some pathetic wife.

XXXVII
Oh, do you mask your sorrow,
While playing the coquette;
Yet, curse events that lured you
And fill you with regret?

XXXVIII
Was ever there a trollop
Who welcomed each embrace?
I'd guess that every harlot,
Has suffered great disgrace?

XXXIX
Your work inflames the lecher,
By daylight or by night.
In alley or in palace
You represent a blight!

XL
Disdain's concealed by smiling.
Your laughter masks contempt.
Dismiss him, oh, so quickly.
Another you must tempt.

XLI
'Tho many names you carry,
There's none suggesting praise.
You're 'trollop', 'slut' or 'strumpet'
Unto your final days.

XLII
I've seen a dozen word forms
And then a dozen more;
But, none with favored meaning.
They all mean, simply, 'whore'.

XLIII
They place you in a penthouse,
With 'call girl' as your name.
Your role remains unaltered.
You're whoring just the same!

XLIV
Yours is a heartless world,
Made meaner as you age.
You've never earned your value,
No matter what your wage.

XLV
Were you first hired for teasing;
But soon compelled to bed?
Were you once thought alluring;
But, now you're shunned, instead?

XLVI
One day you'll be abandoned.
You see this as the truth:
The pimp demands full service,
But only in your youth.

XLVII
Are you serenely happy
Attired in sultry mesh,
And serving nameless mongers
From Minsk to Marakesh?

XLVIII
Or do you join the chorus—
The largest in the world—
'Though each one rendered voiceless;
In fear and hunger curled?

XLIX
Your maidenhead is shattered!
Your fate is understood.
You're damned to play the harlot
'Though years from womanhood!

L
To paint the fullest picture,
There's this that we must say:
The pimps were always sleazy,
Unto the present day.

LI
Your job is not to linger.
Each touch demands a price;
So, take your fee and hustle.
Dismiss him in a trice!

LII

Do strumpets, with their talents,
The stable marriage mar?
Do wives who harbor wisdom
Compete in home's boudoir?

LIII

Your dignity's abandoned
As you perform your chores;
But, none are so pathetic
As some old playboy's whores.

LIV

While I've no love for harlots,
The sisterhood of shame;
I also curse your clients,
Who fuel this heartless game.

LV

Your work inflames the lecher,
By daylight or by night.
In alley or in palace,
You represent a blight.

LVI

For men who dislike women,
Bordellos are the place
To humble and demean them;
To bully and debase.

LVII

Whores learn, through brutal treatment,
To yield and to obey.
All slaves aren't bound in shackles;
Some wear the negligee.

LVIII
How numberless your sisters,
Who shuddered and who cried!
How many were the helpless,
Who protested and died?

LIX
Sick men, who abhor women,
Will sell their sisters to
Sick men who abhor women.
Immoral revenue!

LX
They number in the millions
These girls, whose lives are lost.
Through abject degradation;
Dead souls compound the cost.

LXI
The slaughtering of harlots
Gets very little time.
We rarely give it notice.
It's such a common crime.

LXII
You know that all who visit
Don't seek the self-same thrill.
While some seek warm caresses,
A few are there to kill.

LXIII
The evidence of slaughter?
Their bodies or their bones,
On hills and farms and woodlands,
And bloody cobblestones.

LXIV
Sick lechers go on cruises,
Across the Asian sea,
To find defenseless children
Who are denied a plea.

LXV
Misogyny's abhorrent.
It crafts an earthly hell,
Which goes beyond the brothel.
The home can serve as well.

LXVI
All pregnancy's unwelcome
In that most loveless world.
They need to 'off' the offspring.
Each fetal life's imperiled.

LXVII
How often were you battered,
And seized with mortal fear?
Were you, in truth, enamored,
By someone's severed ear?

LXVIII
If I seem both condemning
Yet saddened by your fate,
Please know your life's two-sided,
So, I equivocate.

LXIX
Don't hope to tame the sadist
With wiles, or smiles you've worn.
Too many of your sisters
Will never see the morn!

LXX
One needs to damn the madam
Who hawks her sisters' skills.
Inspired by lust and money,
Enriched by callous thrills.

LXXI
How many fallen females—
Whose work destroys all pride—
Have tried in desperation,
Attempts at suicide?

LXXII
"Regard for ev'ry human,"
A concept early taught.
How then can sex be sexy,
Coerced, or forced, or bought?

LXXIII
Just who and what protects you,
From brutalizing wrath?
The next, who pays your keeper,
May be the psychopath!

LXXIV
Regarding pimps and panders,
There's this that we must say:
Each one is ever sleazy,
Unto the present day!

LXXV
In some lands, laws permit it:
The sale of human goods.
That doesn't void the stigma
Of damning sisterhoods.

LXXVI
I cringe before the millions
Whose cries we won't admit;
Pulled, sobbing, from their childhood;
Hurled into whoredom's pit!

LXXVII
Or do you join the chorus—
The largest in the world—
Though each is rendered voiceless,
In fear and hunger curled?

LXXVIII
The British relished dunking
Their witches, scolds and whores;
Yet men who trade in trollops,
The universe ignores.

LXXIX
All whoring brings depression;
It burns my tongue to say:
It's one more deathless hydra
That none will ever slay.

LXXX
Now think of all your sisters
Who hate the trade they ply.
Yet few will try to free them
Or hear their muffled cry.

LXXXI
With whores by gate or temple.
Or international mart,
The purity of races
Was blemished from the start.

LXXXII
Three crimes of wicked mankind
Stay ever in the fore:
The curse of wretched slavery,
Plus harlotry and war.

LXXXIII
The world's awash with females,
Whose lot they can't defy;
Whose cries are left, unheeded;
Whose tears will never dry.

LXXXIV
When Nipponese went warring,
With bayonets and guns,
They kidnaped girls and women
To serve the empire's sons!

LXXXV
The records ever censored,
Of kidnapped females doomed
To brutal degradation,
In cheerless rooms entombed.

LXXXVI
"Were they confined to brothels,
Thus doubly damned by war?"
Not brothels, Ma'am; but rap'ries,
From Seoul to Singapore!

LXXXVII
Throughout this wretched planet,
Great mobs should show their rage;
But, none hear muted harlots.
We've other wars to wage.

# WHEN PRAISE BEGINS TO PALE

There's sweat upon my weary flesh
And flies sit there to bite.
With other serfs, I till the land
While waiting for the night,
To give my body vital ease;
To rest my soul a mite.

But even though the Sun's retired
And gloom's upon the vale,
The parson wants a bench repaired.
The master needs some ale.
Aye, they and others, endlessly,
On my good will prevail.

I'll not refuse to do their will—
'Though well, of course, I might—
'Cause somewhere I was taught to aid.
It's proper and it's right.
Our manor has so many needs
And serving is my plight . . .

That's why I work without reward
And give of time, my own.
That's why I help a hobbled man,
His dulling scythe, to hone.
That's why I fix the village bridge,
While toiling all alone.

And many are the skills I use,
While poverty I curse.
And many are the praises gained,
But my lament is terse:
Oh, all those feathers in my cap
And nothing in my purse!

# ULYANOV

The advocate of terror, he
Who chose "N. Lenin" for his name.
From Simbirsk, on the Volga's bank,
To Kremlin's lithic walls he came.

Though many victims soon were slain,
His icy logic he employed
To say, "No omelet can be made
Unless some eggs are first destroyed."

For many decades, terror-filled,
Around our hapless globe arrayed,
They've trampled eggs with frantic zeal;
But, have not one damned omelet made!

# THE RENEGADES

With pain we face the sorry facts:
Some firemen torch; some clergy sin.
Police sometimes do lawless acts;
But, journalists cause most chagrin.

They're unreserved. They aren't sedate.
They write to pummel and to bruise.
They're members of the Fourth Estate
And they manipulate the news.

How savagely they chastise those
Who question what they write or think.
Their friends will feast on honeyed prose;
Their critics drown in printers' ink!

They feel that homage is their due
And they require complete respect.
They'll flay the public figure who
Might fail to fully genuflect.

They claim to push unfettered speech
And raise their banner, all unfurled.
Yet, facts they slant and truth they breach;
They are News Butcher to the World!

They print whatever tweaks their brain
And censor what they damned-well choose;
Since thought control is their domain
And they manipulate the news.

Trade secrets they will keep, untold.
They hardly ever let it slip,
That they defame with bias, bold;
And they will lie by censorship.

What legislator doesn't dread
To challenge their distorted views?
They'd soon unbutter all his bread,
'Cause they manipulate the news.

They praise themselves unto the skies,
Pretending to deserve no less.
'Courageously' they exercise
Their twisted *license of the press!*

# VINTAGE HOTEL

Drab walls, with yellowing white paint.
One wall papered . . . and peeling.
Cracked plaster and transom air.
The bathroom's better . . . perhaps.

A rubber stopper in the sink.
The tub, old before Attlee.
Bare bulb lighting a bare room.
Back to the bedroom . . . again. . . .

Here, we'll observe our honeymoon.
Her robe, draped over a chair.
She wears only a peignoir . . .
Crimson and gauzy . . . waiting.

What a charming place!

# SONNET TO A REFORMED MONGER

*Selection.*
*Affection.*
*Erection.*
*Connection.*
*Infection.*
*Complexion!*

*Inspection.*
*Detection.*
*Injection.*
*Injection.*
*Injection!*
*Correction.*

*Reflection . . .*
*Rejection.*

# ON FLEET STREET

*Say: what pay ye for poems?*
A tuppance and a hug.
*And what pay ye for essays?*
A shilling and a shrug.

*But, what pay ye for falsehoods*
*That titillate the mob?*
Enough to buy a timepiece
With matching gilded fob.

'Though, if your mind is fertile
With lies to fill a tome:
Enough to buy a mansion
And make of it your home.

Our readers pay for rubbish.
Our works are most uncouth.
We thrive on fetid falsehoods
And that's the sorry truth. . . .

# A RAUNCHY TUNE

In Ulster, up in Ireland's north, was where he fell in love.
It seemed her warm and honeyed voice was as the turtle dove.
She was, to him, a warm refrain, this Londonderry maid;
A ballad of sweet baudiness, with form so well displayed.

Whene'er she walked, her backside would monopolize his gaze;
A symphony of joy to him, to occupy his days.
Oft' her posterior he would pat, emboldened by her smile.
He thought their song would last fore'er; but t'was for just awhile.

For she, one day, just ran away, and traveled o'er the sea.
Full soon he heard, with saddened heart, in London now was she.
In hot pursuit, he too sailed forth, across the Irish Sea;
A bitter chantey on his lips . . . a sorrowful melody.

He walked the streets of London town, from dawn to dusk to dawn;
But could not find his serenade; his medley now was gone . . .
From Charing Cross to Hampton Court; from Soho on to Kew,
He eyed each lass, from bottom up, but saw none that he knew.

And, last I heard—though years have passed—he seeks his
    maiden fair;
Still searching . . . hoping . . . to regain . . . his Londonderry Air!

# THE NOCTURNAL COLONEL

There is a Kentshire cottage
Beneath a roof of thatch.
It sits alone, and lonely,
Within a verdant patch.

That rare and rustic dwelling
Is choking in its vines.
You'd guess the place was empty,
Until a lantern shines.

There's a lancer in that cottage,
Who's very seldom seen.
They say he's now retired
From service for the Queen.

He served long years in jungle
And on a river's bank.
He rose in task and title
To earn a colonel's rank.

The colonel's not low stature;
But really isn't tall.
He has a name, folks tell me;
But, one I can't recall.

He's never seen in daytime
As one just might surmise;
But wanders forth in darkness.
It seem's light hurts his eyes.

Each night he walks the byways,
A lantern in his grip.
A corncob pipe he's puffing.
No saber's on his hip.

His brows are thick and bushy
Above his eyes of blue.
They touch each time he's smiling
(A thing he loves to do).

His soldier's cap still crowns him.
His shirt is drawing tight;
But, now it's missing buttons
That popped during the night.

His sideburns, too, are bushy
And just a tad too long;
But, as he strolls the landscape,
He whistles on a song.

He speaks to all the creatures
That cross his nightly path.
His mellow voice discloses
A man who feels no wrath.

When something scoots before him,
To scamper o'er his boot,
He calls, "Now don't be hasty,
My spotted little newt!"

A great owl goes a-swooping
Across the colonel's head;
Then perches on a tree limb,
While owl-speak words are said.

"Just who are you t'whoing?"
He asks with upward glance.
"T'is you I am t'whoing;
Your evening to enhance."

A change in the aroma
Soon settles on the land.
The colonel looks for colors:
Near black, with whitened band.

"Oh, howdy, Mr. Polecat.
I see you waddling by."
"Oh, Colonel, let me tell you:
I think you're quite a guy.

"And have you an opponent,
Who's gotten out of hand?
Just tell me who the target . . .
I'll spray on your command!"

The colonel smiles, but briefly,
Then shouts unto the skunk,
"Since must'rin from the army,
My foemen's list has shrunk."

Then, as the skunk goes waddling,
Beneath a stand of ferns,
The colonel jerks. He's startled.
A tomcat he discerns.

The feline's black as onyx
And blends into the night.
His eyes, alone, reveal him
The colonel feels some fright.

The vet'ran soon recovers.
He'd scared the tomcat, too.
Then both regain composure
And mutter, "Oh! Adieu!"

The black cat bounces boldly
And leaps into the brush.
The colonel puffs with gusto
And whistles as a thrush.

Of course, no thrush comes flying.
They stay anest at night.
The vet'ran sees a nighthawk
Grab insects while in flight.

"Your tastes are very bat-like.
At dusk you both go fly,
And fill your tiny gullets
With bugs that happen by."

Whene'er the colonel pauses
(With lantern, too, at rest),
The moths will hover closely.
Against the glass they're pressed.

Then, as he lifts his lantern
And totters on his way,
The moths all flit and flutter
In utter disarray!

Another group of insects
Are active through the night.
The colonel stops to watch them.
Each has a private light.

"Hello, my sparkling fireflies,
Whose needs are brightly served.
You seem forever rising."
The colonel thus observed.

He strides across a meadow
And then into a wood.
He has so many neighbors
Who share his neighborhood.

The ever-smiling colonel
Had wandered through the night;
But, now, he is returning
Before the morn's full light.

The last friend he'll be greeting
(A doe now fully fed),
Returns to piney needles
That serve her as a bed.

The sky is oh, so rosy:
It's signaling the dawn,
And telling things nocturnal
That darkness is withdrawn.

The kind, nocturnal colonel
Arrives before his door.
He turns, to savor briefly,
The world that lies before.

At last the smiling colonel
Undoes the wrought-iron latch,
And steps into his cottage,
Beneath the roof of thatch.

# EARTH'S AT THE WINTER

*(Rhyming scheme and meter borrowed from the Scottish bard, Bobby Burns.)*

Centuries passing,
All hates fed on gall.
Leaders bombasting;
All missiles then hurled.

Corpses amassing;
But, no roll to call.
There's no recasting.
The firestorm's unfurled!

Earth, too, is passing;
Man crafted the pall.
God's everlasting;
But, shunning the world.

# I LOVE THE LIGHT

I love the light when shadows stretch
Across the fields, as Dawn's begun;
Before receding, hastily,
Beneath the awesome, rising Sun.

I love the light the shower brings,
Reflecting on the dampened leaves,
Or sparkling in the droplets of
The webbing which the spider weaves.

I love the light when fog descends
To rest within the narrow vale,
Embracing weathered country sheds:
Obscuring rustic pump and pail.

I love the light which filters through
The haze of Autumn's dewy morn;
The light which shimmers on the pond
And plays across the sheaves of corn.

I love the light when early flakes
Give hint that winter has begun;
A light that's dim upon the land,
As though a chill o'ercame the Sun.

No matter how the Sun's revealed:
In all its forms, I love the light.
Yet, just as much, when day has gone . . .
I love the darkness of the night.

# THE THINGS WHICH KILL

When blinded Polyphemus chose a rock
To hurl at bold Odysseus in his flight,
His weapon was as one from cave-man's stock;
Its simple function: death to expedite!

But, even then, in that gray, Dorian dawn,
New ways had been designed to maim and slay.
The things which kill have ever come and gone,
'Though killing's stayed in fashion to this day.

Creating weapons always leads the field
Of scientific areas of advance.
New, shining missiles are today revealed,
As genius takes a military stance.

But, whether made by genius or by fool,
Each weapon's still a gross, barbarian tool.

# AN EVENT TO LAMENT

The war has gone away.
Who will we bomb today?

Without a formal fight,
What homes can we ignite?

How will we stay in shape,
If we can't kill and rape?

Without campaigns to win,
What medals will they pin?

Should peaceful times prevail,
We'll all be whole and hale;

But, grit we can't display.
The war has gone away. . . .

# THE MIDDLE OF NOWHERE

Tell me: Where is the middle of nowhere?
Is it deep in a vast alpine range?
Do the mapmakers miss
Its fog-shrouded abyss?
Are the flora and fauna quite strange?

Tell me: Where is the middle of nowhere?
Is it far beyond some ancient sea?
Is it worthy of note,
As a place so remote
That it knows neither law nor decree?

Tell me: Where is the middle of nowhere?
Will you kindly respond to my plea?
If you'll just point the way,
I will go there today;
Because, that's where I'm yearning to be.

# A RHYMING DISCOURSE ON HAVING THE GOOD SENSE TO KNOW HOW TO PROPERLY USE BREVITY IN THE FASHIONING OF POETIC WORKS

My belief?

Keep it brief!

# URGIN' THE VIRGIN

Oh, we push for our daughters to skip childhood play
And we think we must dress them just like Jon Bonet.
We can't wait for their youth to be over and done.
We deny them their childhood of innocent fun.

We buy glamorous clothes to show off our young girls
And we'll spend what we must so they have sexy curls;
Even though we all know there's a risk to think of,
For some stranger might prey on the child that we love.

Fam'ly chats that are bold really give me the chills;
Just admit that you're hunting vicarious thrills!
Yes, the message is simple, I've put with this tune:
*Please don't force our young girls to be women too soon.*

Nature gives ev'rything its own ripening time,
So stop urgin' the virgin from childhood sublime.
God did not make young girls to attract and allure,
So stop urgin' the virgin before she's mature!

# THE ABERRANT ONE

We are ten, and with things which we all yearn to do.
Yes, all ten have set tasks which we want to pursue,
So that I, as a carpenter, hanker to build.
Here's another who farms, and has grain to be milled.
He enjoys raising flowers and she'll write a book.
He prefers to make war, and her wish is to cook.
This chap would paint signs. She, a family craves.
He, a cooper by training, makes barrels from staves.
Also she, in ceramics, makes vases and bowls.
Thus all ten, with true joy, try to work toward their goals.

But, alas! How disgusting! How tragic to say!
That, of all of the ten, there's but one has his way!
He's the one who destroys, while the rest would create.
Only he can decide. He'll allow no debate.
So the wishes of many are shattered and tossed,
By the will of just one, who's immune to the cost.
As good neighbors, we work in harmonious style,
'Til tranquility's smashed by one neighbor . . . most vile!

# LOVE ENOUGH

Yes, I'm a Hindu lover Sir
And I love Nordics, just as well.
I am a Negro lover, too;
And ev'ry Semite, truth to tell.

Plus ev'ry Oriental type
And natives of the U.S.A.
And Eskimo and all the blends,
Such as the oceans' grand array.

Perhaps I've got a malady;
A trait that's ever here and done.
Simplistic, yes; but very true:
I love God's people, ev'ry one.

What need to justify this trait?
This observation's not profound:
When prejudice is kept at bay,
There's love enough to go around!

# SECOND HARVEST

"WE ARE AT WAR!" gazettes proclaimed.
An enemy was boldly named.
We donned our uniforms to train
And learned to crawl through barbed terrain.

How quickly other nations armed
As placid peoples were alarmed.
Then, scared as Hell we sailed away
To gather in a distant fray.

The battlefield became our home;
With trenches as a catacomb.
Gray daybreak was our time to kill.
The sergeant's order harsh and shrill!

The Reaper had been occupied;
By twilight's pink we saw who died.
How many comrades made the list?
Who will be next? Why was I missed?

Some left us rhymes. They wrote them well:
"In Flanders Fields," "The Bells of Hell."
Bad wars produce good songs and books;
As gnarly branches make fine crooks.

No one's designed a proper trench;
With depth enough to quell the stench . . .
The stench we daily stirred afresh,
Of Sulphur . . . gas . . . decaying flesh!

Just as a scandal's rumor flies,
Until all hear . . . and then it dies;
So, too, one morn, a rumor flew,
Until all heard; and then we knew.

The whispered word inspired release.
Years facing death; we now faced peace. . . .
Our weapons tossed on scattered piles,
We looked about with tearful smiles.


The decades tumbled. Pages dropped.
The hourglass grains have never stopped.
In recent years I cringe with age.
I'm but an elder; not a sage.

Our uniforms—threadbare and quaint.
The muster's call is growing faint.
The Reaper stalks o'er field and fen.
He's out conscripting, once again.

More comrades—daily—miss the call.
Soon, there'll be none; no one at all.
The second cutting of the grain
Will cut each stalk, 'til none remain.

My arms and armor won't suffice.
I hear the rattling of the dice—
Dice that the Reaper has recast—
So this campaign will be my last. . . .

# A BAKER'S DOZEN HAIKU

In order to confound the triskaidekaphobiacs, we herewith present thirteen poems modeled after the Japanese *haiku.*

Since the days when Kyoto was their culture center, the Japanese have had a particular type of poetry that we know as Haiku. The most noted haiku poet was an early one, Basho, Haiku is a unique form of poetry that does not necessarily rhyme; but is significant for it brevity and form. The most common form of a Haiku poem has just three lines and but seventeen total syllables.

The poem has a first line of just five syllables, a second line of seven syllables and a five-syllable closing line. It may or may not have a title. Here follows just thirteen of this author's efforts at creating Haiku. The reader might well enjoy penning a few haiku for him– or herself.

# Cycle

The silkworm's astir.
I dream of glorious fabrics
When cycles conclude!

# Hopelessly Lost?

We are ever lost!
Why can't we find the river?
Ahh! There's the fogbank!

# Penniless

Yes, I'm insolvent;
But, thriving in penury,
With friends as my wealth!

# Prolonged Punishment

The chastised child cries.
Long after it stops crying,
My sadness lingers.

# Unwelcome

Ripening chestnuts.
Neglected too long; new life
Wriggles through their skins . . .

# A Visitor's Discovery

Korean Temple;
Source of a hillside freshet
Where faithful tossed coins.

## Lacking Logic?

Murder victim lives!
But, why the lighter sentence?
Failure rewarded?

## The Fourth Deadly Sin

Might ye envy queens?
Should ye learn of Anne the Brit . . .
Envy turns to dust!

## Old Faithful

The wait seemed endless.
Suddenly, a steaming fount!
We raptly proclaimed!

## They Prey

Alone, I'm living,
While telemarketers prey.
Damn them all to Hell!

# Deluge

Rain . . . and flowers bloom.
Rain . . . and rivulets widen.
Rain . . . and floods consume!

# Tribute

Nippon's rhymeless art . . .
Capturing Nature's splendor
In timeless haiku.

# Shame

Poem rejected.
An invalid count was found.
Seppuku's my fate!

FROSTY APPLES

Herewith, a verse;
Concise and terse:

In Wintry time,
My pomes all rime.

~~~

# RELATIVE TIME

"How it flies!" said the conquering Romans,
Offering comment on Time's rapid pace;
And they've now made a clock run by atoms,
Just to measure Time's passage through space.

Now, if life can flash by in an instant,
And the earth, in a twinkling, will burn;
Oh, then, why does an hour seem eternal,
While I'm waiting for you to return?

# STRENGTH

There's a rule we should all glean from life:
Thoughtful men, who are strong, avoid strife.
Weaker folks they respect.
They don't harm; they protect,
And they NEVER hurt children or wife!

# VOICING THE OBVIOUS

When all the smoke has blown astray . . .
And ev'ry grave a corpse contains;
When all the blood is washed away
By cleansing rains . . .

The curse remains.

Despite the signatories' ink
On new accords which promise peace;
And arsenals that briefly shrink,
They're futile gains!

The curse remains.

We know we can't undo the dead.
We cannot free what Death arraigns;
Nor save the blood already shed.
Despite our pains . . .

The curse remains.

Though peace awards might reassure,
Inspiring some to persevere;
In fighting wars there is no cure
For bloody stains.

The curse remains.

We need no bloodshed to remind
Each generation of the gore.
Let's not repeat each act, unkind.
Play no refrains.

The curse remains!

# RHYME OR RUSE?

To one poetic practice end,
I must, with raving vigor, vow
To wage a winning war, somehow!
It does, too many folk, offend.

I don't expect to cope alone. . . .
To triumph takes the toil of all.
Consider this the clarion call;
And find some friends who've spirit shown.

Why, it's a damnable disgrace!
Against this, let us all align:
Alliteration asinine.
Let's put it in its proper place!

# BY NATURE?

Grandparents gray
And haulers dray;
While donkeys bray
And prelates prey.

# A RUSTIC PUZZLE

Now, heretofore, I'd never sung
About the time I found a tongue.
It was a lamb's tongue; that I knew.
But, where the lamb . . . and where the ewe?

And where the ram that sires the stock?
And where the shepherd? Where the flock?
No, just the lamb's tongue's all I saw.
There was no head. There was no jaw.

'Though on the ground, not far away,
There was a lamb's ear, clear as day.
Again, no shepherd and no lamb;
But, just the ear. No sire. No dam.

If this confuses, as it might,
Here's some advice, to set you right:
First pick a *botanist's* sharp brain;
Then have a *carpenter* explain.

If you're still puzzled, as you read;
*A lambasery's what you need!*

# AFTERMATH

Left lame by some forgotten war,
And far too old for muster's call,
I hobbled forth toward battle's roar
To watch compatriots fight and fall.

'Tho slaughter raged 'til setting sun,
My countrymen had won the day.
Invaders saw their plan undone
And quit the field in disarray.

I watched the vanquished slowly leave
And listened to their mournful tune;
A song of hell, without reprieve,
For those whose death had come so soon.

Defenders, too, toward home now turned;
A dazed and daunted remnant few.
No ordered march could be discerned.
They formed no ranks; passed no review.

There was no joyful vict'ry cry.
The victors, too, had paid the cost.
The victors' dirge was also sad . . .
Just as the dirge of those who lost.

As both had countless warriors dead,
So both had wounded near the same.
(Perhaps they'll ask me to command
This ghastly army of the lame!)

Fast-rottng corpses now abound.
Dead souls are left to hold the field.
They'll not contest this trampled ground,
Where pools of blood are now congealed.

The bodies, pierced by sword and spear,
Lie staring o'er their ghoulish realm;
Yet their rule, too, will disappear
As conq'ring maggots overwhelm.


When years have passed, some epic lay
Will sing of naught but val'rous youth.
I hope I've died before that day
And hear it not . . . I know the truth.

# THE DIPLOMATS

We stood beneath the chestnut tree,
In haze before the dawning Sun.
Nine squirrels . . . crouched,with threat'ning teeth;
And I, with cradled, threat'ning gun.

The prize to which we both laid claim
Hung heavy on the tree above.
The chestnut harvest was profuse;
With savory taste I'd grown to love.

I knew my rifle was unmatched;
But they had numbers, which I feared.
We'd both be bloodied in a fight;
And yet, a bloody showdown neared. . . .

Just then I thought, *Negotiate!*
I might survive this duel unscathed,
If both would yield, so both could gain.
A flag of truce I promptly waved.

They watched as I laid down the gun;
They pondered my pacific plan.
They soon unfluffed their bushy tails
And op'ning strategems began.

As table for our crucial talks
I then proposed a wooden block.
"That's inappropriate," they shrieked.
"We must employ that large, flat rock!"

I couldn't let our fragile truce
Be sidetracked by their rodent guile;
So, I agreed to use the stone
And saw, at last, a squirrel smile. . . .

I offered them an even share
Of all the harvest from the tree.
They scoffed at each new offer made.
With each new plan, they'd disagree.

The squirrels' claims remained intact.
The Sun would pass its zenith; but
They wouldn't alter; wouldn't waive
Their claim to ev'ry single nut!

I felt a panic grow within.
Could I accede with any grace?
As fireflies rose, I yielded more,
So fearful that I might lose face.

As ev'ning closed, accords were signed.
I wince at terms my mind recalls.
Those rodents got the chestnut crop . . .
And I got all the prickly hulls!

# GETTYSBURG

Does your town wish for revenue
To prime its economic pump;
To vitalize a sluggish trade
Or overcome a modest slump?
Invite two armies to compete
In nearby fields or village dump.
Then, when the slaughter runs its course,
It's time to play your morbid trump.

First, scatter leaflets to the winds
And set up shops (museums, too).
Get local writers to expound,
While artists smear the crimson hue,
To punctuate the gory scenes.
Then hawk to tourists passing through
(Nostalgia sells so well, these days).
You'll have unending revenue!

"Beneath this oak the wounded lay—
Some lacking limbs; some without eyes.
And here a sniper felled his man:
A major shouting vict'ry cries!
And, here, a non-combatant fell."
An extra, modest fee now buys
A chance to touch the bullet hole.
Thank God for Jenny Wade's demise!

Now rhymesters never should intrude
Upon the poems which they plan;
But, Damn! Why must we turn a coin
On ev'ry bloody act of man?

# THE RODENTS

There are lice in the hairs of their dirt-covered skin,
So they scratch as the crouch 'neath the ground.
Through the burrows they scurry, and squeal in their fear;
Through the maze in the earth where they're hopelessly bound.

They're not mice, though they scamper and run just the same.
They're not rats, though the plague they will spread!
They're not lemmings, though all could be led to their deaths;
And not rabbits, nor squirrels, nor the shrews that we dread.

There's a world above ground that is healthy and clean;
But that's only for *humans* to share.
So they thrive in the stink of their own filthy wastes,
Far too mindless to know; too conditioned to care!

And they sleep in the filth of their stench-laden nest,
'Til a shout puts their rest to a stop!
*"Get yourselves out of bed! Grab yer gun and let's go!*
*'Cause at dawn we will all be going* "Over the top!"
[The preceding lines are based on the trench warfare that was one
aspect of the madness of the First World War.]

# THE QUAKER QUERY . . .

DID
    WILL
        PENN'S
            PEN
                PEN
                    WILL
                        PENN'S
                            WILL?

# THE EIGHTH DAY

I shrank in fear whene'er I thought
Of posing questions to You, Lord.
For years I harbored queries, God;
But, fearing Ire, they were ignored.

But then a thought, to me, occurred:
Two questions others had addressed;
One in the Bible's op'ning lines
And one from Calv'ry's Cross was pressed.

"Am I my brother's keeper?" Thus,
Cain's query, steeped in mockery.
The second of despair was born:
"God, why hast Thou forsaken me?"

With both those questions, asked of You,
*Jehovian Wrath* went unrevealed.
This spurred my eagerness to ask
Of troubling doubts *I've* long concealed.

I see no truth that's truer, Lord,
Than that which I'll elucidate:
*Each act of fav'ritism sows*
*The seeds of jealousy and hate!*

Your Heav'nly fav'ritism, God,
I'll challenge to my closing breath.
The seeds You planted in his mind
Inspired Cain's rage . . . and Abel's death!

Cain saw Your fav'ritism, God;
A treatment he could not abide.
So Cain, *the first from woman's womb*,
Committed murder: fratricide!

(In sim'lar vein, was Joseph seen
To be his father's favored son.
This led to moments in a pit
Before long exile was begun.)

Lord, why are men Your favored group,
With women but an afterthought?
Why not from Adam's robust heart?
Why from his rib were women wrought?

Why send a Son to save mankind?
Why not, in pairs, Your Grace allot?
Why did You give a Son, alone?
Why was no Daughter so begot?

How easily we men took charge.
We made the rules and penned the scrolls.
With wants of women brushed aside;
We held the purse and set the goals!

They're but the vessel of man's seed
(Six thousand years, by Ussher's date.).
Six thousand passive, servile years
Have women walked with humble gait.

If force destroys her maidenhead—
A major trauma in her life—
Why, then, *compound her sorry state
By making her, her rapist's wife?*

Why is Your corps of Angels kept
Confined to men throughout the Book;
Yet, women fill grand earthly roles
In ev'ry cranny; ev'ry nook?

Females are told: "*You must obey*,"
(Though mates may be as tyrants, true!).
Their fate is cast: It's servitude,
For husbands "shall rule over you."

*No human* should be placed in thrall.
All bondage reeks of wickedness;
Yet women were but pawns of war;
Mere tools controlled by orn'ryness!

Poor females, so innately kind;
Gentility, their sweetest trait;
Why, God, are they so oft enslaved;
Their entire lives' in thrall to hate?

Both weak and winsome, they've endured
The carnal acts of loveless mates;
And when they bear their bastard young,
They're banned to life beyond the gates!

When men go forth (*as e'er they do*),
To conquest that is oft' unjust,
Females, of varied age, are jailed
In rap'ries for their conq'rors' lust!

Lord, when You drowned all human folk—
Except for eight—beneath the tide
And only four females survived,
Why weren't those four identified?

And why, in Sacred Passages,
When Angels' roles are there supplied,
Are females absent from The Text?
*Just as on Earth, they're brushed aside!*

In op'ning pages of the Book,
A flawed Creation was implied,
When You beheld Your handiwork
And sought *repair* by genocide!

O' why the Flood *and why the ark?*
*Why did You drown all souls*, worldwide?
Why were the innocents unspared
*And why no Mercy e'en implied?*

Within the Sacred Scriptures, Lord,
I find not one informing verse,
Supporting ancient Noah's bane;
His vile and baseless filial curse!

Yet, millions suffered servitude,
Controlled by stinging whip and rod;
Condemned by Noah's wicked tongue,
Tho' never, ever, damned by God!

I searched the Sacred Passages,
Then searched them thrice again . . . and well;
But, found no base for Noah's curse.
Might *anyone* curse one to Hell?

So Noah, long upon this earth,
Condemned a guileless, blameless heir . . .
As well the damned one's progeny?
No tyrant's plot is more unfair!

Mere *birth* brought chains to Noah's damned.
Their bondage but a wicked perk,
While Noah had three centuries more
To view his heartless handiwork!

Will ev'ry one who agonized—
All those enslaved when Noah cursed—
Earn hefty, Heav'nly Recompense;
Their withheld Glory, reimbursed?

Say, how improve on humankind
If basic flaws are left intact
And all the violence increased,
While all the virtues are attacked?

What craftsman, who designs a work;
But sees some flaws that merit shame,
Will then discard the shoddy work
Yet start anew *with flaws the same*?

Your broader fav'ritism harmed—
Let's note it well, in language terse—
Your favor, shown to but one tribe.
That's *Israel's e'erlasting curse!*

You told the world, "I favor one;
The tribe I'll favor evermore!"
The world replied with brutal acts
And scattered them to ev'ry shore!

Why did You favor but one tribe?
Unequal sharing truly glares!
All tribes are Your creation, God.
Why can't all tribes hold equal shares?

Please. Hasten to reclassify
All acts of choosing favored kin—
Or playing fav'rites anytime—
And label each a *mortal sin!*

If fav'ritism's made passé,
We'd squelch distress before it flares.
We'd see an end to jealous rage
Of greedy heiresses and heirs!

Since Ever is eternal, God,
I ask of You a special tweak.
Please add, Dear Lord, just <u>*one more day*</u>
To Your inspired Creation Week.

May I impose, another time,
To ask of You a favor small?
Could You, *post-haste*, inform the world
That sexual preference was *Your* call?

From ancient times until today,
From data any soul inspects:
A share of women and of men
Were fully drawn to their own sex. . . .

Aren't all the spectrums in our world—
All those in which we oft immerse—
Your handiwork, O' Timeless Lord;
Throughout our total universe?

All spectra are of Your Design;
From simple to the most complex.
You've varied light and heat and hue.
You've varied strength and sound and sex.

From ancient Lesbos' olive groves,
To San Francisco's turbid bay . . .
Your Sexual Spectrum's been in force . . .
A force that lingers 'til today!

Your utterance would soon dispel
The rumors and the verbal flood
That caused so many painful words
From parents to their very Blood!

Another question comes to mind:
Oh, why impound our backlogged souls?
Why hold our souls for endless days?
Who'll get the Bliss and who the coals?

Why has Your Son not yet returned?
What has delayed the Quarters planned?
Why hold Your Judgments of the dead:
The *welcomed souls* or *spirits banned*?

Is Armageddon's clash foretold?
Will You, *triumphant*, sound the knell?
If Satan is at last subdued,
Won't Hades' *threat* be gone as well?

Recall this universe's birth
Just six full days and it was milled;
But, twenty centuries have transpired
With Heaven's Quarters yet unfilled.

I beg . . . implore . . . entreat you, Lord!
Please, Lord . . . Just one creative date
To make small tweaks for humankind
To tide us o'er as we wait. . . .

Please add to your Creation, Lord—
In your Creator's Lasting Role—
A valued feature that we lack . . .
A *conscience* for each human soul!

Yes, add a *caring conscience, God,*
In all new folk whom You create.
Let human hearts check Satan's will.
Your earth will turn; but be sedate.

Please fuse a *conscience* to the heart
Or as a pairing with the brain;
To give mankind a grand restart.
T'would ban the haughty and the vain!

If we all housed a *conscience*, God,
Our meanest word and cruelest deed
Would not transpire to foster pain
Or ugly viciousness to breed.

The mayhem would disintegrate!
Farewell the bloody battlefield!
Abusive speech and stinging words
To pleasing, gentle phrase, would yield.

No more the predatory pain.
No more the tyrant's heartless grip.
No more humiliating acts.
Let's toss the shackles and the whip!

Could You, Dear God, take on that task
Within a glory-filled eighth day?
Our gratitude would justify
The Grace and Love that You'd display.

Our brain is quite the wonder, Lord;
Our sight's a splendid, marv'lous tool;
But what we need as well, Dear God,
Applied throughout: Your Golden Rule!

I'd forfeit all my tenure, Lord,
In Your Own splendid Paradise,
If You would make one modest change;
One deftly anatomic splice.

How easily you'd then attach
A grand device for doing good;
The *conscience* ev'ry human lacks.
True kindness would be understood!

And further, if I may, My Lord:
Is Armageddon in our fate?
And, can the outcome be assured?
If "Yes," why do You wish to wait?

Why not confront and conquer Hell?
Why not release the world from Hate?
Millennia have come and gone
And yet we watch . . . and still we wait.

So, if You'll tweak Creation's world,
I beg of You a final toil.
Configure well the faunal gut,
So all life feeds upon the soil!

A soil-based diet for this earth
Would end the carnivore regime
And, thus, create a gentler world
Without predation in the scheme!

I worry, too, about Earth's end . . .
Will You and Satan fight no more?
Have secret protocols been signed
So Both can thrive, forevermore?

Lord, will we need a Judgment Day—
If Satan's crushed—to set us free?
Can't Mercy be applied throughout,
So ALL Your Children dwell with Thee?

Of those who never heard Your Word
And those who would forever doubt?
Will they, in darkness, ever dwell;
Or will Your Mercy pluck them out?

Will You be merciless until
Our very end upon this ball?
Won't Mercy reign on Judgment Day
As You give Joy to each and all?

"Just follow me or perish!" is
The raging tyrant's card'nal threat.
I can't believe that You'd condemn
The doubter to prolonged regret!

I can't believe that You would damn,
To *outer darkness* evermore,
All those who never knew your Grace
Nor knew t'was You they could Adore!

'Tis most unseemly, I'll declare,
For those who first embraced Your Call,
To badger dying skeptics when
Your Boundless Grace should welcome all!

As Thomas doubted, so do I.
Must we be damned and hobbled low?
Won't You accept our ling'ring doubts?
*Once in Your Presence, all will know!*

Is there no room in Heaven's Halls,
For *doubters* with their modest lapse?
We know that, once admitted There,
All *doubts* will crumble and collapse!

Though You began this World, Dear Lord,
By fav'ring Abel and his kin;
Might You please hold Your Curtain's fall
And welcome *ev'ry* soul within!

Dear Lord, Your Mercy I beseech.
You know I'm *timid* to the core.
Let me, on Earth, fore'er reside.
This Globe's the Gem that I adore!

Please close this world to Glorious Chords!
Let Grace enfold all souls who seek.
Swing open Heaven's Gates to *most* . . .
But, Know that I'm among the meek!

# PRIESTLEY

The Humbria's a waterway
In Albion's north countryside.
For land beyond its northern bank
The name, Northumberland, applied.

Some bold Northumbrians set forth,
As local fortune turned unkind.
They traveled t'ward a distant land.
But kept their homeland's name in mind.

Where rivers join in ageless flow,
In Pennsylvania's virgin stand,
The trav'lers found their haven-site
And christened it "Northumberland."

The town took root. The settlers thrived,
Enjoying profits from their stake;
While back in England lived a man
Who was to follow in their wake.

Our subject was a Yorkshire man—
A linguist, preacher, scientist, sage—
A man of letters and of thought;
Exceptional in any age.

When not involved in rev'rent cause,
He'd study gases freshly found,
Then write his thoughtful monographs,
And, on their properties, expound.

When his exper'mentation seemed
To reach the point of no advance,
Two lab companions would step forth:
The studied hunch and happenstance.

His isolated oxygen
The Lords would have done well to share,
To puff their speeches on the floor
With dephlogisticated air!

Conviction made him speak of change,
But some find change a fearsome threat;
So he, and other thoughtful men,
Were scathed and scorned and much beset.

With chapel burned and house defiled,
He moved to London for a spell.
Unwelcome there, he chose to sail.
Northumberland is where he'd dwell.

Far safer is the raging sea
Than where a riot may occur.
One's homeland is no longer home
With primal ignorance astir.

They watched another century turn
Before the Yorkshire genius died;
His corpse interred—and yet remains—
In William Penn's fair countryside.

He balanced well, within his thought—
And so his writing indicates—
True Science and Religious Faith;
Those two elusive counterweights.

So, speak a word on his behalf
When some conforming soul complains.
'Though nonconformists are condemned,
They parent most of progress' gains.

A prophet, says a sacred verse,
Is shunned within his native land;
But, whether he was shunned or praised,
The Priestley legacy will stand.

# INTERLUDE

The following two rhymes hark back to an earlier era, to what is now known as "Biblical times." The "Middle East" wars are among the oldest in human history. They involved Assyrians, Egyptians, Hittites, Cannanites, Hebrews, etc. Herewith, a pair of rhymes that reference that ancient era from whence a phrase developed about "wars and rumors of wars." This pair of selections is not meant to identify which side or sides are responsible for *today's* lingering agony in that tiny, but crucial, segment of the globe. They are simply meant to suggest that ancient legends linger and can be used as source materials for modern poetic reflections.

# URIAH, THE HITTITE

Young Uriah, the Hittite, a soldier became
In his bride's native land (old Judea, by name).
There he fought for King David, who ruled from above.
There he served with a loyalty greater than love.
While Uriah defended the realm and its king,
David first saw Bathsheba (a ravishing thing).
Royal lust and desire would disrupt many lives
(Can a man know of *love*, with a full fifteen wives!).

'Though Bathsheba was wife of Uriah you know;
Yet did David adore her, his loins all aglow!
Now since kings, just as commoners, sin may condone,
Young Bathsheba was brought to the palace, unknown.
T'would be nice if the record reluctance described;
But, we truly don't know if she had to be bribed.
As their indecent coupling, their marriage, defiled;
She would soon inform David that she was with child.

When he knew that their scandal would now be revealed,
David ordered Uriah's return from the field.
To Uriah the Hittite, sealed orders he gave,
To be given the captain, king's honor to save.
They would kill the young groom in the battle storm's eye,
For a king without conscience; a wife who'd not cry.
So Uriah was gone . . . as the Hittites are gone.
But, the arrogance of the example lives on.

Now fair Palestine's cast in Bathsheba's old role;
While the Zionists clearly evoke David's soul.
With the refugees sacrificed, out on the sands,
Would that someone could give us what Justice demands!

# 1948

In Palestine, a ghost observes
Two armies, as they war.
'Though both are ancient to the land,
New weapons cause new gore.

The spectre, looking on the scene,
Looks not at warring men;
But, watches saddened refugees,
Who flee as best they can.

Although they suffer in their flight,
They hold a glowing yen:
They hope that they'll go home some day;
But, know not how nor when.

The ghost—who is a Canaanite—
Has seen it all before.
He moans: "They've done it once again;
Just as in times of yore!"

# THE PHOENICIAN PORTS
OF OLDE

The Phoenician ports of Olde?
Ah, is that your question, Sire?
Why, if I may be so bold,
They were Byblos, Sidon, Tyre.

From the one our Bible's named,
For the books that were, there, sold.
And for trade was Sidon famed
(Homer's rhymes about that told)."

But, the third, so we have found,
Feeling Alexander's ire,
Was soon leveled to the ground,
To be Hist'ry's first flat Tyre!

# POEMS

I suspect I'll never see
A tree as lovely as an ode.
Rhymes are so easy to transport;
But, trees, alas: they must be towed!

The tree, its hung'ry roots, has pressed
Against the earth, as I recall.
Those self-same roots which, all too soon,
Thrust up to make my mower stall!

While ev'ry Autumn one can find
My poems shelved in tidy dress;
Yet, my small lawn, so acid-drained,
Is always one great leafy mess!

I yearn to be a poet, great;
That's if I ever had a choice;
But, since I don't, I must admire—
For now, just plain old Kilmer, Joyce . . .

# WHO SPEAKS FOR THE WARTHOG?

We watch the lioness a-stalking;
The warthogs are their common feasts;
But, lions aren't the kings of wildness;
We *humans* are the royal beasts.

The warthog, soon consumed by terror,
Goes racing, vainly, o'er the veldt.
Full soon, the lioness is clamping.
The warthog's fate is brusquely dealt!

The lioness sinks claws and canines.
The warthog's desp'rate cry is shrill;
A plea for aid, that goes unanswered.
One final squeal . . . then all is still.

Compassion? Why none for the warthog?
Yes. Why refuse to recognize?
Are we too tired to raise a digit?
Are we too cold to empathize?

Malevolence is near pervasive.
Widespread compassion's overdue.
While fetuses squirm, unprotected,
The forceps grips, and rips, on cue.

Who gives a damn for unborn humans?
With our barbaric rules applied,
We let the ghouls control the clinics
And we won't stir for *feticide!*

# ADVICE TO AN ABORIGINE

Does your rude hut look dull and drear,
Appearing tired and tumble-down?
Then hard repairs you cannot shun.
Repelt the side; re-cap the crown!

And on the walls you must put bark
With pitch, or something sticky, up.
I promise it will then look new.
That's how to wake your wickiup!

# FOR LOVE

*(To the tune of "Simplice," by Tchaikovsky)*

Let's steal away,
To someplace where we can love;
Where breezes are cool
And passions will rule,
While stars glitter high above.

Let's steal a kiss,
A kiss that goes on and on;
With boldness that grips
Our hungering lips,
While night fades into the dawn.

Let's find a nook
Where I'll be alone with you;
Just hidden away
An hour or a day;
Or maybe a week or two.

Let's dare to dream:
A dream that we'll make come true.
We'll welcome the chance
To make our romance
A love that is always new.

Let's take a vow
To live, evermore, as one.
With light from above
We'll make the white dove
The symbol for all we've done . . .
For love.

# THE SOLEMN SWEARERS

When presidents declaim their oaths
And utter to the fawning crowd,
The nation looks, and glows with pride.
Each native heart is justly proud.

But, we all know—if we'll admit—
The luster pales; the pride recedes.
Each spotless one self tarnishes.
Our leader changes as he leads.

We might expect each aspirant,
The august office to besmirch.
We seek for men of noble mien;
But, that's an almost futile search.

In fact, we've gone the other way.
The ones that voters let survive,
Not chancing image newly stained,
Are tarnished well when they arrive!

# QUAKER LADY

I feel no breeze, and yet I see you shake;
So delicate you are, so slight your stem.
Though frail, you thrive. Imposing trees don't break
Your will to flourish; small, blue, flowering gem!

In early Spring you looked like ling'ring snow.
I should have known it was your clustered bloom.
You'll grace our fields for months before you go;
Mid-summer's heat will fin'ly be your doom.

We'll miss you through the long ensuing days;
Recalling other names you've garnered, too:
Like "Innocence," reflecting naïve ways;
And "Bluets," from the palest shades of blue.

When next the snow's departure we discern,
We'll watch, to softly herald your return. . . .

# THE PRIZE

She, the white woman who taught in the village.
He, the wild warrior, eas'ly tamed by her eyes.
They lived together, apart from their people.
Yes, they lived as outcasts; but they had the prize.

They saw the glances, the looks and the hatred.
They sensed the meanness that pure envy inspires.
Then each would look in the eyes of the other
And they would smile, knowing they had the prize.

Each day they thanked their Creator and Maker,
While enduring the pain from the meddlesome lies.
Each gained more strength from the love of the other;
Still sharing a smile, knowing they had the prize.

Sadly, by moonlight, some bigots attacked them,
Thus, leaving the couple to face their demise.
Weakly, each searched for the eyes of the other.
Tho' dying, they smiled, knowing they had the prize. . . .

# PSALM OF AUTUMN

Hear the soft crunch of twigs as we're walking.
Now the honking of geese breaks the calm.
A chill wind has the branches a'talking,
Harmonizing, in Nature's great psalm.

We are moving in Nature's own setting,
While absorbing its spirit and life.
Nature suffers no loss in the letting;
With that essence all nature is rife!

We've concern that the leaves are a'dying,
As the green turns to crimson and gold.
We feel sad, and we find ourselves sighing.
We despair of the oncoming cold.

But, recall! Nature's ever renewing.
She will always return new for old.
So our gloom we would best be subduing;
And rejoice as the seasons unfold.

Yes, the leaves of the forest are dying;
And the trees are, with color, alive!
All that color, which Autumn's applying,
Is God saying . . . that all will survive!

# THE ROMANCE OF WAR

Our young should know of war:
That pre-historic way
Men found to wound . . . to slay . . .
To smear the land with gore!

Our young should early learn
That slaughter can be done
To groups, as well as one;
No mercy to discern.

It might be well to teach
That twisted minds delight
In barbarism's sight;
'Though claims to 'order' preach.

To help our young ignore
The horror and the hell,
We've made a myth, and well:
The fine romance of war!

This knowledge to bestow,
We should with passion yearn.
War's TRUTH our young should learn;
But war they should not KNOW!

# SHAM ROCKS

I spent two years a' searchin'
From dawn t' dusk t' dawn,
Before I fin'ly found one:
A wily Leprechaun.

Two decades more I've hunted,
O'er ev'ry inch o' ground.
A sober son o' Erin?
'E's nowhere t' be found!

# THE WALL OF NAMES

Most walls are built to separate;
But, this wall's made to bind.
It brings together fallen souls
With loved ones left behind.
This wall will span the ocean's waves,
This wall will span the years;
And, though it sheds the pounding rains,
It will absorb the tears.
I watch, as others place bouquets.
I hear them softly cry
While making tracings of the names.
They hope, the same as I.
We pray . . . and hope to capture here,
By tracing out the name,
The spirit of a loved one lost,
That we can hold and frame.
Our son, they said, stepped on a mine
That lay beneath the ground;
But, no remains were gathered then,
And none were ever found.
They never sent a body bag.
No "welcome" could occur.
We held a dismal service; but,
With nothing to inter.

So I, too, trace my hero's name.
Upon the sheet it's pressed.
And, if I've caught his troubled soul,
I'll take it home to rest.

And when, someday, we put aside
All campaigns, great and small,
We'll know the world has finally learned
The message of our wall.

# RECOMPENSE?

I write poems, both lengthy and terse.
I've submitted them: good, poor and worse.
There were some which they used:
But, to pay they refused.
Ah . . . so that's what they mean by 'free verse'!

# PRUNING

I'd hardly thought the task would be
So difficult to do.
I'd hoped to soon the discern the best;
But find that that's untrue.
But, I shall have to persevere
And do the job at hand.
To choose the best; reject the poor,
'Though taxing the demand.

We'll cut this one, on Mother's side;
Town drunk for all his life.
And here, Dad's uncle has to go;
He had the foreign wife.
Out goes the banker cousin, too;
The old embezzler one.
Out, too, the pauper lad, as well;
And Aunty's bastard son.
Now, him I like; he owned a mine
And all the workers, too;
And him, and her, and her and him:
An 'educated' crew.
We'll keep the uncle, he who owned
A thousand city flats;
And Grandma, with the mansion huge;
Despite the filthy cats!

We must discard the student, too;
The radical, you know.
As well, the Bible-thumping one;
He's simply got to go!

This one's a bum; and she's a crook;
And he's a little strange.
These people can embarrass so.
Their flaws can reach full range!

There's so few left; but, we'll make do . . .
Make do with what we've got . . .
Once we've discarded all of those
With names which tend to blot.
I've done the work. Results are slight;
But, now, at last I'm free.
The quality's all there. Behold!
A lovely family tree!

# PECOS BILLIE

Oh, I met my True Love, and I want you to know,
Down in Villa Nueva (VEE a noo AVE uh) in New Mexico.
She was born by the Pecos, where cool waters run
And her pa named here "Billie," expectin' a son.

Pecos Billie's the law in this sun-covered land.
Pecos Billie's the lady now wearin' my brand.
I was sentenced to make her my unblushing bride;
Well, I never could run and I sure wouldn't hide!

'Though she carried no weapon, she came to no harm.
Billie disarmed the toughest with beauty and charm.
On the banks of the Pecos her law was the best
And my poor heart she quickly placed under arrest!

Well, my heart soon surrendered, with nary a fight.
On the banks of the Pecos one warm summer night.
She would never use handcuffs; but, still, I'm not free
'Cause I can't break these heartcuffs that she placed on me!

Yes, out west of the Pecos, true love is a tort,
So I threw myself onto her merciful court.
We took vows in a mission that sits high above
And today I'm a lifer, for Billie, My Love!

# NOCTURNAL CHANGE

When spring arrived, we saw a doe,
A female rabbit, at the edge
Of our rear lawn, hard by the ridge,
And 'neath our poorly tended hedge.

A later time, while hacking weeds,
I spied small rabbits in a nest
Which she had burrowed for her young.
I moved away, unwanted guest.

In recent weeks we watched them grow
And roam our lawn, so unafraid;
Although we'd see their startled jumps
When sudden noises had been made.

The ridge is where they settled in;
Where brush and briars hide the ground.
But, still, each morn they would return,
To nibble grass and hop around.

Last night we heard the foxes bark
And shuddered at a sound so mean.
Today we looked—but looked in vain!
The friendly rabbits can't be seen. . . .

# BATTLEFIELD REUNION

Here we meet, don't you know? Comrades now without foe.
Here we camp and recall battle scenes.
Now we sit by our tents, to compare past events,
As we feast on a soup made with beans.
Here we laugh and we sing while we have us a fling,
For tonight we will not have a care.
Yes, the kettles will steam and old comrades will beam,
While the mem'ries of combat we share.
So, we mingle with pride and take aging in stride.
Soon our spirits are fully restored.
Of our nation we brag and salute us a flag;
Then we pause to give thanks to the Lord.
But, I voice my dismay at the closing of day,
As we rest under moon's gentle light:
Should we not shed a tear for dead comrades so dear,
Who still haunt our old campground tonight?

# BITTERSWEET NIGHTSHADE

You know we met upon a stony hill,
Beside a cornfield, on my morning walk.
Your stamens full and as a golden bill;
Lavender petals on a pale-green stalk.

'Tho time would pass before I learned your name,
And then your toxic nature I recalled.
As medicine, your berries held mild fame;
More often—as a poison—you've appalled!

You sell the lesson well, that all should know:
That many things in life are well to seek;
But, all things, in excess, bring sad return
Unless, of course, t'is Love of which we speak!

'Though your forbidden berries make us ill;
I'll still consume your beauty at my will!

# HOMELY FORECAST

Evening red and morning gray
Sets the traveler on his way;
But, evening gray and morning Red;
Brings down terror on his head!

# I HOPE YOU SEE

At the village well's where he first met me
And we chatted there, 'neath a date-palm tree.
Which is nigh, I'd say, to the Galilee;
Although rather far from the old Salt Sea.

"With our taxes high, I'm glad water's free,
As tradition says it must always be."
Thus, I spoke to him; but he'd disagree.
"Ah, tradition's not for the likes of me.

"I'd so like to yield; but I'm Sadducee."
I responded here, seeking clarity:
"But, if anything, you seem filled with glee."
"Oh, I'm happy, happy as one can be:

"But, the fact remains that I'm Sadducee."
Here we ended our baffling repartee
And I thought for hours, 'til it dawned on me!
Until then, of course, I was sad, you see!

# RECOMPENSE?

I write poems, both lengthy and terse.
I've submitted them: good, poor and worse.
There were some that they used:
But, to pay they refused.
Ah . . . so that's what they mean by 'free verse'!

# ONE POEM PENNED

I penned a poem so obscure, I knew not what it said.
I'd planned to rhyme each second line; but left them blank, instead.
The lofty theme within my mind, the paper never saw.
I could not write two lines that worked. No image could I draw.

But, 'though it was inscrutable; as vague, as vague can be,
I sent it off, with all my rhymes, an editor to see.
Perhaps I needn't end my tale; you likely sense the tone.
The editor returned them all, except that one, alone!

# INTESTATE

And, now, I lay me down to sleep;
I pray the Lord my soul to keep.
If I should die before I wake,
The state will, all my treasures, take!

# THE APRON

In our kitchen she reigned; a benevolent queen;
Although no royal cape on her shoulders was seen.
'Round her waist was an apron of white, trimmed in red;
Not of ermine of course; but of muslin instead.
There were too many duties she couldn't omit;
But her housekeeper's apron helped ease them a bit.

With her apron she wiped the spilled stew from the pot;
And she used it to carry a pan that was hot.
She employed it to open a jar, tightly sealed,
Or to carry some freshly-picked fruit to be peeled.
She wiped flour from her hands when she baked us our bread.
From our cheeks she wiped most of the tears that were shed.

Now it's faded and frayed; a few stains it displays,
As it hangs on the peg, near the stove where it stays.
Alas, decades of time, their sweet victim have claimed,
Leaving subjects to mourn and successor unnamed.
'Though our sovereign is gone now, for nearly a year,
Her old apron might yet . . . wipe away . . . one more tear!

# THREE MOTHERS

Three mothers crowd my pensive mood
As Mother's Day arrives.
There's little else my mind can hold,
Than thoughts of those three lives.

All three have had to sacrifice.
Each one some pain has known.
All three have had to struggle on,
And each has cried, alone.

But, loving's what they've all done best;
That love their offspring knew.
Compassion's how each one expressed
Her love, as children grew.

As Mother's Day arrives this year,
I'd honor, here, all three:
My mother, wife, and daughter, dear.
A rose to each of thee!

# CARTOUCHE

Upon the scented bond I pen you name,
Then look on it with warm and loving gaze.
The sight of it brings pleasure to my heart
And offers respite, brief, from Love's malaise.

But, something leaves me troubled at the sight.
It's not quite adequate just as it stands.
There's something more required to make it right.
It seems there's some adornment it demands.

No extra stroke or flourish will suffice;
It must be some especial sign I make.
No, not because your name's not fine alone;
But, rather, simply, for your beauty's sake.

Why not the old cartouche from pharoah's land . . .
The oval that enclosed the royal name?
You are my queen, and yes, you are my quean;
And for both roles I love you yet the same.

So, 'round the word I draw the constant line
That lends your name a touch of the elite.
I look once more with adoration's gaze,
For now, at last, your name looks quite complete!

# NAN

Of course, there is sorrow
And, yes, there are tears
For you, who grew sweeter
Through all of our years.

Your smile ever lingered;
A joy I now miss.
Although you grew weaker,
Pale lips blew a kiss.

This pen I'm discarding,
Our match to renew.
I'll soon be abiding,
Forever, with you. . . .

# NIMROD

"And the hunter home from the hill."

Tis' Stevenson's line I recall;

But, the pen has replaced the quill . . .

And the hunter's home from the mall.

# OWED TO ALCOHOL

A thousand times I must have heard
What I presume is Wisdom's word.
That driving, after one's imbibed,
Can earn someone a stone, inscribed.
I've also heard, in private talk,
That drinkers sometimes cannot walk
And those who use unbridled drink
Will also lose the power to think.
But, more than these; yes, most of all,
When all its sadness we recall,
To this we can, our seals, affix:
That DRINKING/LIVING DO NOT MIX!

# ONOMATION

The swishing of a skirt
And thumping of a drum.
The harpies shrieking wail;
The Onomates will come!

The hissing of the viper
And sloshing of the beer;
The tap, tap of a finger,
The zinging of a spear.

The frying bacon's sizzle
And bump, bump of the coach;
The chugging of the engine,
The Onomates approach!

The screeching of the owl
And tinkling of a bell.
The Siren's lilting call;
The crackling flames of Hell!

We hack in anxious tension
And whimper in our fear.
Our words are slurred and raspy . . .
The Onomates are here!

# THE GREAT WALL

Across ten thousand hills it snaked its way
And, as the largest structure ever made,
Yet stands, a muted monument, today,
To organizing genius there displayed.

T'was built, we're told, to benefit all those
Who'd live in later centuries . . . safe . . . secure.
"A life was spent for ev'ry stone that rose."
A price quite small to keep a culture pure.

But, when the Khan desired his Hordes sent forth,
Sung land was as a pantry filled with ants.
The thousands ran, with ease, out of the North,
To clamber o'er the Wall in their advance.

One must conclude: It simply wasn't built
To help protect the peasant or his land;
But, to maintain a dynasty in gilt,
Against a fearsome Mongol warrior band.

We'd hope a lesson might from this be learned:
'Tis wrong to sacrifice someone today,
For benefits presumed, once night has turned;
'Cause Fate may change all factors on the way!

Too many structures have been dearly built,
On footings made of human flesh and frame;
Some structures are of architectural tilt.
Far worse are those political in name.

In recent years, in that brave land so old—
That land where Wisdom's said to have been born—
More innocents have died, a million-fold;
While loved ones, by the hundred millions, mourn.

Digest, then, one small truth, Friend, if you can:
Do not abuse frail life for any plan!

# FOREORDAINED

Aye, ev'ry tale of love—

Those past and those yet pending—

Are doomed to end the same:

Each has a woeful ending. . . .

❀ ❀ ❀

# ABOUT THE AUTHOR

Guy Graybill is the author of a half-dozen books, published by Sunbury Press, and has also had articles and poems published in a variety of magazines. One book and several poems were also published in England.

A widower, Guy has been a resident of Snyder County for most of his life. Following three years of military service, he got a degree in History from Gettysburg College and became a teacher in Middleburg Pennsylvania. He also obtained graduate credits from Temple, Bucknell, Pittsburgh, Puget Sound, and Georgetown.

Graybill has been a county commissioner and has contributed more that 150 pints of blood at drives of the American Red Cross.

Forewords for three of the above books have been written by a Pennsylvania Secretary of Education, an opera singer, and a presidential speech writer.

His very varied poetry subjects form the basis for this volume.

www.ingramcontent.com/pod-product-compliance
Lightning Source LLC
Chambersburg PA
CBHW030933090426
42737CB00007B/413